D0057142

A *GIFT* of the
MISSION VALLEY
FRIENDS OF
THE LIBRARY

Praise for *What's Your Story?*

"*What's Your Story?* chronicles the art and science of storytelling, the most effective communication device used with various degrees of success by societies and individuals since the beginning of time. Authors Ryan Mathews and Watts Wacker are not only gifted historians and futurists, but articulate storytellers as well, making this, their second collaboration, a delightful read for a wide audience. I was so fascinated by their insights in how companies and individuals tell their stories that I bought copies for all of our executive leadership team and for my spouse and children as well. None of them were disappointed and all have started honing their skills by using the advice offered by the authors in this clever, well-written book.

"Three thumbs up for *What's Your Story?* Three thumbs? That's another story."

—Bob Rich, Chairman, Rich Products Corp., Author *Fish Fights*,
The Fishing Club, and *Secrets from the Delphi Café*

"As usual these two future-finders have their fingers on the pulse of what's happening— and what we need to know about. In every business, in every organization, the seven most important words these days are: 'But wait! A story goes with it!' You need to read this book to find out why."

—Alan Webber, Co-founder, *Fast Company* magazine

"A great story sparks our imagination, challenges us to think, and resonates with our collective conscience. Ryan Mathews and Watts Wacker's story about telling stories does exactly this. It is an essential guidebook for capturing and conveying the essence of corporate identities and enriching brands."

—Paul A. Laudicina, Managing Officer and
Chairman of the Board, A.T. Kearney

"There is an old Irish proverb that translates into: 'Listen to the sound of the river if you want to catch a fish.' *What's Your Story?* is the ideal way to listen to the marketplace, and readers will find the fishing there to be both fun and profitable."

—Senator Feargal Quinn, Seanad Éireann (Irish Senate)

"Everyone enjoys great storytelling, whether in a book, movie, or play. Ryan Mathews and Watts Wacker have now applied the art of storytelling to business and provided us with tools and examples that show us how stories can strengthen our brands, companies, and industries."

—Kimberly Till, Chief Executive Officer, North America, Taylor Nelson Sofres ("TNS")

"I loved this book. It was witty and irreverent, and totally relevant to anyone in business today, regardless of discipline. Everyone likes a good story and the business lessons in *What's Your Story?* will resonate with everyone."

—Lisa J. Donahue, Managing Director, AlixPartners; Executive Vice President and Chief
Financial Officer, Calpine Corporation

"This book is a must-read for marketers, brand managers, marketing students and, more globally, for anyone interested in understanding the emotional attraction/repulsion effects brands have on us.

"A lot has been written on brands; however, this is the first book to analyze branding through the original angle of 'storytelling.' Ryan Mathews and Watts Wacker make a brilliant demonstration showing why and how a great and emotional story is one of the key success factors of a strong brand.

"The Walt Disney Company has elevated this branding strategy based on storytelling to an art. Every Disney animated movie tells a great story, which is developed into a standalone brand. Each product featuring the movie characters contributes to telling the same story and acts as media delivering brand awareness and, ultimately, building brand equity."

—Dominique Bourse, Co-Chairman and Co-Chief Executive Officer of Cyber Group Europe and former Senior Vice President, The Walt Disney Company (Europe)

"My take: This book reinforces the sometimes forgotten notion that a great story, told by a great storyteller, can capture and transport thinking to a new place and a new perspective. When done well, it is an instrumental tool in propelling the audience toward getting the correct point. Anyone in the business of conveying, communicating, and convincing should take note."

—Tom Zatina, President, McLane Foodservice

"Today, businessmen, mothers, teachers, lovers, politicians, and more are communicating around the world with the stroke of a keyboard or touchpad. What is lost in this method of communication is the essence of the message, some critical fact, the true meaning, or even the intended tone of voice. Mathews and Wacker point out in their wonderful book, *What's Your Story?*, that storytelling's origins go back thousands of years and is an art that passes through entire civilizations. Stories often span generations and are immensely powerful in shaping the perception of an individual or an organization. Mathews and Wacker detail what it takes to be an effective storyteller.

"Connections made through stories often lead to richer personal and business relationships and give a clearer understanding why a certain path was chosen. Mathews and Wacker entertain the reader and cite numerous examples of how past and present notable people have cultivated a public persona that was different from their personal lives. I, for one, will never think of Walt Disney the same.

"Even at an Internet startup like eBags.com, which launched in 1999, new team members almost a decade later soak in stories about how the company started in a living room, survived on credit card debt, and faced seemingly insurmountable challenges, including the dot.bomb and the 9/11 tragedy. And as eBags has expanded to Europe and Japan, stories of the frugal early days play a key role in grounding new eBaggers into the company culture. On a personal level, my story of surviving a deadly cancer directly led to the life-changing realization that I wanted to co-found the world's largest online retailer of bags."

—Peter Cobb, Co-founder/Senior Vice President Marketing, ebags.com

ALSO BY RYAN MATHEWS
The Myth of Excellence

ALSO BY WATTS WACKER
The 500-Year Delta
The Visionary's Handbook

ALSO BY RYAN MATHEWS AND WATTS WACKER
The Deviant's Advantage

WHAT'S YOUR STORY?

FT Press
FINANCIAL TIMES

In an increasingly competitive world, it is quality
of thinking that gives an edge—an idea that opens new
doors, a technique that solves a problem, or an insight
that simply helps make sense of it all.

We work with leading authors in the various arenas
of business and finance to bring cutting-edge thinking
and best-learning practices to a global market.

It is our goal to create world-class print publications
and electronic products that give readers
knowledge and understanding that can then be
applied, whether studying or at work.

To find out more about our business
products, you can visit us at www.ftpress.com.

WHAT'S YOUR STORY?

STORYTELLING TO MOVE MARKETS, AUDIENCES, PEOPLE, AND BRANDS

Ryan Mathews   Watts Wacker

SAN DIEGO PUBLIC LIBRARY
MISSION VALLEY BRANCH

3 1336 08084 0615

Vice President, Publisher: Tim Moore
Associate Editor-in-Chief and Director of Marketing: Amy Neidlinger
Acquisitions Editor: Martha Cooley
Editorial Assistant: Pamela Boland
Development Editor: Russ Hall
Digital Marketing Manager: Julie Phifer
Publicist: Amy Fandrei
Marketing Coordinator: Megan Colvin
Cover Designer: 4 Eyes Design
Managing Editor: Gina Kanouse
Project Editor: Betsy Harris
Copy Editor: Keith Cline
Proofreader: Karen A. Gill
Indexer: Lisa Stumpf
Compositor: Jake McFarland
Manufacturing Buyer: Dan Uhrig

 © 2008 by Pearson Education, Inc.
Publishing as FT Press
Upper Saddle River, New Jersey 07458

FT Press offers excellent discounts on this book when ordered in quantity for bulk purchases
or special sales. For more information, please contact U.S. Corporate and Government Sales,
1-800-382-3419, corpsales@pearsontechgroup.com. For sales outside the U.S., please contact
International Sales at international@pearsoned.com.

Company and product names mentioned herein are the trademarks or registered trademarks of
their respective owners.

All rights reserved. No part of this book may be reproduced, in any form or by any means, without permission in writing from the publisher.

Printed in the United States of America

First Printing August 2007

ISBN-10: 0-13-227742-5
ISBN-13: 978-0-13-227742-6

Pearson Education LTD.
Pearson Education Australia PTY, Limited.
Pearson Education Singapore, Pte. Ltd.
Pearson Education North Asia, Ltd.
Pearson Education Canada, Ltd.
Pearson Educatión de Mexico, S.A. de C.V.
Pearson Education—Japan
Pearson Education Malaysia, Pte. Ltd.

Library of Congress Cataloging-in-Publication Data

Mathews, Ryan.

  What's your story? : storytelling to move markets, audiences, people, and brands / Ryan Mathews,
Watts Wacker.

     p. cm.

  ISBN 0-13-227742-5 (hardback : alk. paper) 1. Marketing. 2. Storytelling—Economic aspects. 3.
Corporate culture. I. Wacker, Watts. II. Title.

  HF5415.M3365 2007

  650.1—dc22

                                                                         2007005372

To my four favorite stories—Gabriel, Adam, Sierra, and Zack.
I can't wait for the next chapters. And to Priscilla,
who proves that happy endings aren't just in fairy tales.

—Ryan Mathews

This book is dedicated to Mr. Richard (Dick) M. Clarke, who was
the original source of inspiration for its inception, and to my dad,
Watts Wacker (himself), who taught me the power in storytelling.

—Watts Wacker

CONTENTS

Contents

Contents

ACKNOWLEDGMENTS

I'd like to thank Tim Moore, who saw our vision for this book, and Russ Hall and Martha Cooley, who kept us focused on getting our story just right.

—Watts Wacker

I would also like to thank Tim, Martha, and Russ for their patience and perseverance. Once again, a special word of thanks to Rafe Sagalyn of The Sagalyn Agency for his sage counsel and firm guidance. As always, a special word of thanks to Priscilla Donegan and our children, who once again suffered through the neurosis of the creative process.

I'd also like to thank Dr. James Clinton who kept body (if not mind) together during a tough physical challenge associated with the completion of this book.

Finally, a note of thanks to the close circle around me: "Mr. Pete" Traskal, Maximum Bob Leahey, Fred Crawford, Jim Singer, Dave Donnan, Patrick Kiernan and Lady Day, Tom Zatina, Mark and Cathy Baum, Jerry and Kate Dunn, and last, but never least, Greg "Greg Z" Czentnar. Special thanks to Rick Kelpin, who has shared my story without question or fail all these years; Richard "Rick" Jackson, still the friendliest face a traveling man can find; Mark Arminski for filling the world with art; and Robert Abate, who's known my story longer than almost anyone, for continuing to play the blues and all that jazz. Spiritual thanks to Steve Barnett and Alan Webber, who continue to influence from afar, and to one and all at Car City Records and Record Time for supporting the habit. And, as always, a wink and a nod to WTB and PTH, but that really is another story.

Finally, in memory of those whose stories are being written in books we can't read yet: Samantha Leahey, Sheila Kelpin, and all the others short and long past who will be remembered as long as their stories are told.

—Ryan Mathews

ABOUT THE AUTHORS

Ryan Mathews, founder and CEO of Black Monk Consulting, is a best-selling author, globally recognized futurist, speaker, consultant, and storyteller. Hailed as one of the few true modern business philosophers, Mathews pioneered the study of corporate cultural ecology. He has been profiled in publications from *Fast Company* to *Wired*. He is the coauthor (with Fred Crawford) of *The Myth of Excellence* and (with Watts Wacker) *The Deviant's Advantage*. He lives in the metropolitan Detroit area.

Watts Wacker is a futurist and founder of FirstMatter LLC, a twenty-first century think tank and ideas foundry. He is the co-author of *The 500 Year Delta, The Visionary's Handbook*, and *The Deviant's Advantage*. He is known for social commentary around the world.

INTRODUCTION

L ong before the first formal business was established, before the first deal, the six most powerful words in any language were *Let me tell you a story.* And, if there is ever a time when the last deal is done and the last business closes its doors, those six words will still be the most compelling anyone can utter.

Businesses tell stories all the time. In fact, we've invented a whole vocabulary just to deal with the kinds of stories we tell. The stories of business are all but endless, but the process of business storytelling is anything but organized or consistent. Let's take a look at the kinds of stories businesses—including your business—tell every day.

There's branding (the stories of our products and services), marketing (the stories of how customers respond to our offerings), and promotion (the stories of how sales of our offerings can be increased). We also use stories for recruitment and, perhaps to a much less-effective end, for retention. Privately held companies often tell stories to bankers or other investors, and one of the most important jobs for a chairman, president, CEO, and CFO of a publicly held company is to tell effective stories to Wall Street, or The City, or whatever their community of financial analysts is called.

There are also the stories businesses tell the media, often in response to stories the media creates, or is in the process of creating, about business; stories businesses tell each other during the merger and acquisition process; and the sad, plaintive stories that less-than-successful businesses tell the courts during bankruptcy proceedings. Businesses tell stories about their past and their futures. The shelves of the Business section of any large bookseller are jammed with the stories of sitting or recently retired executives and the leadership, management, and sales "secrets" of everyone from Santa Claus and Attila the Hun to Jesus and Billy Graham and Colin Powell and Richard Marcinko's "Rogue Warrior."

We said that the process of business storytelling is often unorganized and inconsistent. Let's go over a list of some typical business stories again with an eye toward common inconsistencies:

- We launch a product with a story of how it's the perfect solution for a customer's needs, and then months or years later we "relaunch" it with a story claiming it's now "new" and "improved." What the stories can't explain is how something that has existed for years can be "new" and how you can "improve" on an already perfect solution.

- We go into bankruptcy court and tell a story that "explains" how a company that can't pay its bills in the present has all but unlimited potential in the future.

- We fill the pages of the financial press with stories of how our new CEO will transform the enterprise, and when he or she fails to produce the expected results, we plant a library of stories about how the company will be better off under new management.

- We tell our customers stories about how pricing will never be better, and then six months later offer deeper price cuts and perhaps additional purchase incentives.

- We tell anyone in earshot how good business is, how strong sales are, and how much the customer loves our product or service. We then tell our employees stories of commercial hardship, the necessity for belt tightening, and the inevitability of outsourcing and plant closings.

For years, both together and individually, we've studied, worked with, and consulted with a wide number of businesses across a broad portfolio of industries in dozens of countries.

Our goal is simple: The next time somebody says to you, "So what's your story?" we hope you will have a better answer than you did before you read this book.

*O*nce upon a time before time, the gods of the East, the West, the North, and the South gathered for their teatime to discuss all the things that gods discuss over tea. In between the rather too avid consumption of celestial finger foods, there were passionate discussions of the highest metaphysical sort. Among the topics eternally discussed were such weighty questions as whether it was ungodlike to consider weighty questions and why, if in fact they were gods, they never seemed to be able to resolve weighty questions. It passed what would have been time, if time existed, but the truth was the gods were bored. "Please don't take any offense," said the God of the East, wiping the crumb of his celestial scone from his infinite beard, "but I'm getting just a tad tired of the four of us having these endless conversations."

"I agree," chimed in the God of the North a smidgeon too eagerly as he bit into a cosmic watercress sandwich with exactly the proper amount of mayo.

"Well, what do you have in mind?" asked the God of the South and God of the West simultaneously.

"I don't know," said the God of the East. "We're gods, we can do anything. What if we were to make something besides ourselves?"

At this, the three other gods fell into deep thought. At last, the God of the South said, "I've got it! I'll create a universe—vast, apparently infinite, but tantalizingly almost measurable with a certain physical je ne sais quoi that will keep things interesting."

"Great idea," said the God of the West. "I'll fill it with planets, stars, moons, lots of cosmic gas, spinning masses of rock, and the occasional black hole."

"Well," said the God of the East, not wanting to be outdone. "I'll populate at least one of the worlds with all kinds of creatures—harmless, dangerous, useful, and just plain weird. In fact, just for laughs, I'll create a creature that looks a bit like us—but never so handsome. I'll put him in charge of things."

All the gods had their eyes on the God of the North. "What are you going to create?" they asked in a divine chorus that sent celestial winds roaring through the newly created universe.

"Oh, let's see," he said, stalling for time. "These creatures you've created bellow and bark, howl and cluck, roar and bleat, but frankly I can't understand anything they're saying, if they are even saying anything. I'm going to create language for the creature that most resembles us. That way, they can sing our praises, and when they don't, we can make their little planet tremble, or grow frozen, or cause it to rain on their picnics."

And so, in the beginning there were words, and the words became stories. At first, the creatures the gods called men did what the gods anticipated and used the words to tell stories of the gods and their power. Eventually, however, new stories that glorified men rather than gods began being told. The stories of the gods were told less and less often. But don't worry. By the time men had forgotten them, the gods had all but forgotten men, too. All that remained of the gift of creation was the story.

Chapter 1

THE STORY OF STORIES

Successful companies know that more often than not in business, it really is the same old story.

Or, to be a bit more accurate, it's all about understanding how to use the elements of stories and storytelling to drive business improvement. There isn't a business in the world today—large or small, high or low tech, public or private—that cannot improve performance, internally and externally, through the study and mastery of the basic element of storytelling. One of the most basic applications of this principle is borrowing characters from well-known stories and naming your products or services after them. It works for Paul Bunyan breakfasts in diners across America. It worked for the Atlas missile and Hercules Powder. And, once upon a time, it also worked for a struggling running-shoe company in Eugene, Oregon.

In 1964, Phil Knight was a fledgling athletic-shoe salesman whose career high point had been selling $8,000 worth of imported Tiger running shoes out of his Blue Ribbon Sports store in Eugene. Seven years and $992,000 in annual sales later, Knight unveiled the Nike name and its "swoosh," and the rest, as they say, is history. We're not sure how many of the runners who poured into Blue Ribbon Sports knew that Nike was the winged goddess of victory in Greek mythology, but we're pretty sure Knight knew the power of the story of the original Nike and was trying to tie the critical elements of that story to his brand.

Scott Bedbury, brand guru and Nike's former head of advertising, explains:

> The sneaker was just a sneaker, in every way pedestrian,
> until Phil Knight and Nike came along and connected the
> aspirational and inspirational rewards of sports and
> fitness with world-class innovative product performance
> like that of the Nike Air shoe. Nike could have spent
> millions of dollars preaching the value of encapsulated
> gas trapped within a thin, pliable membrane in the middle
> of the shoe, encased by a molded foot frame and attached
> by a dynamic fit system. Instead, it not only simply *showed*
> the product but also communicated on a deeper, more
> inspirational level what the product *meant* within the
> wider world of sports and fitness. It transcended the
> product. It moved people. [1]

That, in a nutshell, is exactly what great business storytelling is all about.

The Nike story is more than a story of effective branding—it's one of the tens of thousands of stories about how businesses use stories every day to launch brands and enhance the image of existing brands; to train new hires and invigorate seasoned employees; and to help CEOs position themselves in the eyes of Wall Street and aspiring managers position themselves in the eyes of their CEOs. Walk into any Home Depot, and you'll discover brand names such as "Husky" and "Rigid"—frankly, kind of ham-handed branding attempts aimed at men who are either overimpressed with or unsure of their own masculinity. That's branding, arguably at its "best" and "worst." But tying your product or service back to a myth like Phil Knight did is more than branding—it's a rudimentary form of storytelling.

Storytelling isn't just about selling products. Effective storytelling can launch industries. Let's go back to nineteenth-century Vienna, where a young physician by the name of Sigmund Freud is trying to sell, first the scientific community and then the world at large, a new theory to explain all human behavior. He populates his theory with concepts such as the Oedipus and Electra complexes that, like the name Nike, echo back to the ancient myths of Greece. We suppose he could have given these conditions proper Latin names, but if he had, would we have the multibillion-dollar mental health industry today?

Maybe so. Maybe not.

Freud's success proves the ability of a great story to change mass behavior. Sadly, it was a lesson learned all too well by another Austrian—Adolf Hitler—who attempted to weave the future of the German people out of the fraying strands of near-forgotten stories found in the pages of arcane ancient Nordic and Vedic mythologies.

Storytelling has the power to change the destiny of a company, an industry, a nation, and—ultimately—the world. It's a force as powerful and universal as gravity and, sadly, often almost as invisible to the people it impacts. What would you say if we told you storytelling was the most underutilized weapon in most companies' strategic arsenals?

What if we told you that, with very little conscious effort and practice, you could become an effective corporate storyteller? Our bet is that—sooner rather than later—you'd demand a little proof. Fair enough. That's why we wrote this book.

The Da Vinci Code: A Case Study in Effective Story Retelling

Hard as it is to sometimes remember, given all the hype and controversy that accompanies it, *The Da Vinci Code* is nothing more or less than a story, albeit a story that has captured the attention of apparently everyone from the most modest fiction reader to the Vatican. More correctly—and with all due respect to author Dan Brown—it is a retelling of a series of popular stories from the legends of the

Knights Templar and the stories of the Crusades back to the story of the Mother Goddess found in almost every society throughout history. Part of why *The Da Vinci Code* works is that we already know critical parts of the stories before we read them and are preconditioned to accept the argument.

But this "story" has launched an industry whose products include (among other things) a movie; dozens and dozens of books; wall clocks; t-shirts; music CDs; tours, vacations, and travel guides; playing cards; videogames; paint-by-numbers sets; jewelry; diet guides; pornography; and apparently anything else to which you can reasonably, or unreasonably, attach the name "Da Vinci." To make the marketing effort more successful, some Canadian marketers have even altered Leonardo Da Vinci's famous Vitruvian Man—a drawing of a naked man superimposed with an extra set of arms and legs, bordered in a square and a circle—and eliminated the more obvious images of manhood to make sure the image could have greater and broader commercial appeal.[2]

It may be a while before we calculate the full economic impact of *The Da Vinci Code*, but the preliminary results are staggering. More than 60 million copies of the hardcover edition had already been sold before the first paperback was off the presses. Perhaps predictably, the movie version of the story grossed $224 million worldwide over its opening weekend. The value of the *Da Vinci* "industry" is likely to finally settle somewhere between $750 million and $1 billion, a pretty respectable return on assets by anyone's reckoning.

Beyond the Business Case

The Da Vinci Code could have been a fast-selling summer beach book, but it turned into a billion-dollar industry. Why? Because it is a story tied to an even bigger story.

As aging Baby Boomers begin to consider the next stage of their collective lives, dozens of industries from financial services to pharmaceuticals are trying to tell Boomers a story they can relate to. The music—and more important, the spirit of the 1960s—is being invoked in advertising spots for everything from retirement planning to Flomax, a drug designed to improve urinary flow. But it was *Da Vinci* author Dan Brown who, consciously or unconsciously, understood the power of retelling the oldest story of them all: man's relationship to God. It might be easy to dismiss *The Da Vinci Code* as a footnote to American pop cultural history, until you remember it's a billion-dollar brand that represents the tip of a multibillion-dollar industry—an industry every business in America should be paying more attention to. Take a walk around your favorite bookstore, and you're likely to find sections that didn't exist 20 years ago or that have expanded radically over the past two decades. These include Religious Fiction, the Religion section itself, New Age, a radically democratized Philosophy section, and the old stand-by Self-Help titles.

As National Public Radio (NPR) correspondent Martha Woodroof of member station WMRA reported in an "All Things Considered" broadcast on July 5, 2005, "The American reading public is spending lots of dollars looking for meaning in twenty-first-century life." In 2006, the Book Industry Study Group released figures indicating that the Religion category had an 8.1 percent increase in net dollar sales from 2004 to 2005 (to $2.3 billion) and that category sales were expected to increase 6.5 percent in 2006 and 6.3 percent in 2007, sales the industry rightfully views as miraculous in this age of digital entertainment. Some have gone so far as to suggest that the sale of religious books is what's keeping U.S. publishing healthy.

Why the success? Simply put, an aging population—and a younger population facing mass global and domestic instability—desperately wants to be told a story with a happy ending. Religious-flavored stories—whether the apocalyptic visions of the Tim LaHaye and Jerry B. Jenkins's 17-volume and counting

Left Behind series or the gentle ethical messaging of renowned storyteller Andy Andrews—hit a nerve with tens of millions of people who find themselves confused, lost, unhappy, afraid, and—perhaps above all—mortal. The simple story of "believe and you shall be saved" has never played before a more anxious and receptive audience, but it's only one of literally thousands of successful stories you could use to grow your business.

We're not, by the way, suggesting that you need to stop selling trucking equipment or restaurant supplies and begin selling Bibles and fictional accounts of salvation or rename your corporation after an obscure Nordic god of success. Instead, we are saying that understanding an audience, learning what stories they respond to, and then using those stories to "sell" your product or service is an effective positioning tool for any business.

Storytelling and Business

We're willing to bet that your business already engages in a good deal of storytelling.

Creating stories and telling stories are the most universal human activities. An anthropologist might try to tell you that tool making is what separates man from animal, but any decent marketer or brander will tell you it's myth making. Chimpanzees, we've discovered, use tools, but only human beings use stories to explain themselves (and sell things) to each other.

If you had happened to turn on your television set as this book was being written, you might have seen a commercial for the Nissan Pathfinder. Our ears perked up when we heard the ad's tagline—"Discover Pathfinder—tell better stories." A quick look at Pathfinder's website (www.nissanmotors.com/pathfinder) yielded a classic example of conscious corporate storytelling. At the bottom of the screen, a shaded box invited us to explore "Nissan Insider Stories." One click brought us to two other boxes. The first contained a simple phrase: "Everything we touch, we shift. And everything we shift, we make better." The second box invited us to share a deeper storytelling experience. "You will find this mantra at the core of every person who touches a Nissan vehicle," it read. "These are their stories. The memorable, compelling accounts worth sharing. Click and explore each story to experience the shift yourself."

Research in Motion's BlackBerry is another of the many brands jumping on the storytelling bandwagon. The company invites Internet users to visit its "Owners [sic] Lounge" on its website and share their favorite personal story. Tell the right story, and you, too, can become one of BlackBerry's "Success Stories" and have your picture and story broadcast throughout cyberspace.

Why Stories?

Why stories? Again, because stories are the universal human common denominator.

Think about it for a moment. How many times in the past month have you used one or more of these phrases:

- What's the story? (What's going on?)
- What's your story? (Explain your behavior.)
- What's his/her story? (Who is he/she?)
- I don't know the whole story. (I need more data, or don't take what I say as the whole truth.)
- That's my story, and I'm sticking to it. (It's either the truth or as much of the truth as I'm prepared to tell you.)
- What's the back story? (What's the story that preceded this story that helps bring it into focus?)
- Here's the story. (Here is the truth.)
- Nice story. (I don't believe you.)

You get the idea.

In the same way that all of us use the basic concept of stories in a variety of ways in our everyday conversations, businesses use stories and storytelling to perform a series of mission-critical tasks from employee recruitment and morale building to sales, marketing, and branding. Smaller, entrepreneurial firms use stories to sell business plans to banks, and large publicly held businesses use them to sell analysts and investors on the company's direction or to spin bad quarterly results.

Storytelling is so much a part of who we are and how we live our lives that we almost forget about its importance. To borrow a phrase from contemporary pop media culture, storytelling is "embedded" in almost everything we do as individuals and as businesses.

The Myth of Business and the Business of Myth

Despite the role that effective storytelling plays in the success of a business, too many people still think of storytelling as just a form of entertainment without widespread commercial application. On one critical level, business is just another social institution like religion, government, and education, subject to the forces of culture like any other institution. Business even has its own "pop culture," generally expressed in acronyms like CRM, ERP, SCM, and ABC. We like to call the idea that commercial activity operates somewhere outside the boundaries of history, traditional culture, and society, and that it's somehow largely immune to psychosocial forces or anthropological truth, the "Myth of Business."

We're not sure where the idea first caught on that business is somehow a unique human activity subject only to its own rules and driven by the whims of the economic marketplace, modified only by the vagaries of domestic and global politics and regulation. That idea is dangerous. Tap into popular culture or link your business story to stories that already resonate with your target audience, and you're well on your way to success.

Of course, you have to be very careful about how you tell the story. Before a story can be commercially successful, a significant number of people need to be able not only to "find themselves" in it, but also to find themselves in the audience.

Consider the traditional American "health food" store. Its story was simple—eat commercial food, and poison yourself and your family. Eat "natural" and "organic" foods, and expand your consciousness and extend your life. Over the years, rightly or wrongly, the mass market seemed to associate the early health food pioneers with faddists, nudists, cultists, and other fringe figures.

Now consider Whole Foods—the fastest-growing, and by some accounts the most profitable, food retailer in the United States. Its "story" is the same but with a subtle twist. Natural and organic foods are "better" for you. Not only that, they taste better, and you don't have to be a food fascist or organic chemist to shop for them. Not only that, but Whole Foods offers an opportunity to join a community not of food fanatics, poultry paranoids, or culinary conspiracy theorists but of normal, affluent people—folks just like you—who are rightly concerned with the quality of their life and health. Same plot line, but the profits are in the nuances of how the story is told.

Just as there is a Myth of Business, there is also the "Business of Myth," which is to remind us why the notion that business stands outside culture often translates into fatally flawed judgment. We view business as nothing more, and certainly nothing less, than another cultural institution or artifact. We see organized business in the same light as organized religion, organized government, or organized education. As a result, we believe that myth can have the same level of importance and offer the same value to business that it does to any other cultural institution.

By the time the twentieth century ended, the business community found itself rushing toward Y2K, what corporate urban legend held was sure to be a technologically driven Armageddon. It was a time when the blanket woven from the strands of mechanistic industrial metrics—reliance on process and systems over content and imagination, and Alfred P. Sloan's almost feudal conception of the corporation, the template for General Motors—was starting to irrevocably unravel.

Absent the industrial anchor that had defined business for almost three centuries, commercial thinkers and corporate leaders struggled to reposition what it was they did and even how they described their efforts. Some proclaimed themselves engineers of the Information Age, while those on the bleeding-edge of strategic thinking boldly declared the Information Age over and rattled on about the prospects and perils of life in the Post-Information Age. Soon a great deal of business thinking began to suffer from an acute loss of context.

Think of context as a kind of referential frame that not only acts as a border for a picture, but in the process of providing that border actually becomes an integral element in what the viewer sees. Great frames can be works of art themselves, but the best frames accentuate rather than compete with the art they hold. Sometimes frames become so much a part of the piece they surround that, if they were to be suddenly taken away, our perception of the work would be totally changed. In the most extreme cases, we'd no longer be able to distinguish the work from all the other elements in the room that housed it.

At the turn of the twenty-first century, many businesses had effectively lost their context. As a result, the picture they thought they were displaying made sense only when they were looking at it from the inside. To the outside viewer, the customer, the supply chain partner, the competitor, or the analyst, what had once been a clear, representational work was reduced to an image from Jackson Pollock's worst nightmare.

At the very heart of this book lies an idea at once modest, revolutionary, and, for more than some (we suspect), counterintuitive: that mythology, the aggregate collection of ancient stories from cultures around the world, can and should play a critical role in helping resolve many of the complexities and crises associated with the world of twenty-first-century business and society. This is especially true for what we call the Abolition of Context—a phenomenon that negatively impacts every aspect of corporate life, from human resources to product development and from marketing to corporate governance. Modest, because, at its heart, a myth is nothing more or less than a simple story created to convey an even simpler truth or principle.

Don't Blame Us; Blame Plato

The *New Oxford American Dictionary* echoes the popular Western historical bias when it defines a *myth* as "...a widely held but false belief" and *mythology* as "a set of stories or beliefs, about a particular person, institution or situation, esp. when exaggerated or fictitious."[3] Most of us have grown up thinking of myths—assuming, of course, that we thought of them at all—in this context. They were little more than fairy tales of ancient gods and monsters, at best cultural artifacts of interest only to Renaissance artists searching for subjects, Hollywood scriptwriters hopelessly stuck for a time-honored plot twist, and the odd psychoanalytic thinker or two struggling to label a newly discovered neurosis. The "truth" is that this view couldn't be less true. And, the difference between truth and true is the basis of our next chapter.

"*You know, it's true* we've been married a respectable number of years," the old man said, contentedly looking across the sunlit porch at his wife.

"Ain't that the truth," the old woman snorted, the slightest formative traces of a sneer curling threateningly at the corners of her lips.

"Truth is, as I'm thinking about it, I can't imagine how I could have managed to live without you," the old man went on as his gaze trailed away from his wife, focusing on some undetermined point over the ridgeline.

"I 'spect those are the truest words you've ever uttered," said the old woman, her vision turned inside, to near-forgotten memories of an autumn dance now lost across better than six decades.

"It's been a good marriage, and that's the truth," the old man said, now more to himself than to his wife.

"Think that's true, do you?" she whispered under her breath, the words sinking soundlessly into the knitting that lay half finished across her lap.

"Truth is, a man might have done a lot worse than to choose you for his bride," he droned on, his voice softening as it danced back and forth over the thin line separating the last, feeble protests of consciousness from his afternoon nap.

"That would be true if we were talking about a real man," the old woman said, mouthing the words in the folds of her heart rather than saying them out loud.

It was a well-rehearsed routine between the two of them, honed carefully, if not lovingly, for the better part of half a century; the passions of a spring so powerful it couldn't be contained slowly turned into a winter of endless trivial recrimination.

"Tell me the truth," he said as his mind stretched imploringly closer to the sweet intoxication of the temporary oblivion his nap granted him each day. "Have you been happy?"

"Is it true that anyone is ever really happy?" the old woman said, probing the shadows of her memory for a few precious recalled details of the young man not yet grown into the old man who sat rocking across from her.

It was true that, as the years passed—especially the past four or five—it had become harder and harder to recall the slight bend in the nose, that dimpled chin, the hair the color of straw at harvest time (hair that now, despite gallons of carefully applied Brylcreme, seemed to have a mind of its own whenever even the gentlest wind blew). As the days rolled past her, she could remember a piece here, a piece there, but it was as if the truth of him had somehow gone loping down the country road of her memory, kicking up so much dust in its wake she could barely make out its outline, could no longer recall its truth.

"You talk a lot of foolishness," the old woman said, but the truth was the old man was already well beyond hearing, at least for the moment. "True to his nature," she sighed as she picked up her knitting.

Chapter 2

TRUTH STORIES VERSUS TRUE STORIES

"The truth is rarely pure and never simple."
—Oscar Wilde

"Men occasionally stumble over the truth, but most of them pick themselves up and hurry off as if nothing had happened."
—Winston Churchill

How many times have you been sitting at your desk or in a conference room and heard the phrase, "Let me tell you a *true* story?"

We're always curious about his phrase. Does it mean that the other stories the speaker has told you in the past weren't true? Does it mean you should pay more attention to the story because it's been verbally flagged as true? Or is it just that the speaker really wants us to understand how important his or her point is? We're not sure, but we know that a more compelling phrase would be, "Let me tell you a *truth* story."

A story that conveys a *truth* seems like it should be more important than a story that is just *true*. It may be true that somebody sat at home on Friday night because he had no friends, but what are we supposed to do with that knowledge? By the same token, we really don't know whether Thomas Edison actually tried more than 600 variations of filaments before he successfully produced a working electric light bulb, but the truth of that story is that persistence pays off.

Storytelling Lesson Number One:
Stories, Personal or Corporate, Don't Necessarily
Have to Be True to Contain Truth

We're not suggesting that lies are a more effective go-to-market or
internal corporate organizing principle than sticking with the facts.
In general, we'd say honesty, authenticity, and credibility are all
critical elements to great storytelling. When it comes to the true
and the truth, however, we're forced to agree with Plato.

In his *Phaedo*, the ancient Greek philosopher described myths as
truth stories rather than true stories. Plato's theory was that just
reporting facts might tell you what was *true* (that is, what had actually happened), but providing those facts with a greater context—a
story, if you will—was a much more effective way of getting a larger point across.

Enron: Frankenstein and Jesus—Two Ways of Telling the Same Story

You don't have to look much past the headlines in *The Wall Street
Journal* to get Plato's point. Consider the case of Ken Lay, the
founder, one-time CEO, and former chairman of Enron, who died
in July 2006, a fallen idol and broken man.

The "facts" of the Enron case are clear and, at least in business
circles, well known. The company Lay founded in 1985 first
flourished and then floundered, filing for protection under
Chapter 11 in December 2001, following a historic dip in its stock
value. Criminal investigations were launched in 2002. In
January 2006, Lay and former Enron CEO Jeffrey Skilling found
themselves on trial for fraud and conspiracy. Five months later,
Lay was found guilty of 10 counts, and in July, while he was
awaiting sentencing, Ken Lay died of an apparent heart attack.

The "Enron story" will no doubt be studied for generations as one of the classic examples of corporate greed, financial and accounting manipulation, and corruption.

The "Ken Lay story," on the other hand, is the stuff of classical mythology. Lay is the flawed hero of myth who began his journey as the son of a poor country preacher in Tyrone, Missouri, and rose to become, in turn, a naval officer, a Ph.D. economist, a corporate economist for Exxon, a university professor, an employee of the Federal Energy Regulatory Commission, the president of a local Houston-based gas company, the founder of what promised to be the most powerful energy company in America, one of America's highest paid executives, a friend of presidents, and, finally, a convicted felon. Put in the right context, Lay's life and career become a parable illustrating the inevitability of a "fall" when the "hero" misplaces the moral compass he inherited at birth and ends up flying too close to the sun, only to die because of his blind ambition and venturing too far from his original path of righteousness.

So, ask yourself, which is the more compelling story? Which story draws you to it?

Is it the sterile recitation of the facts of the corporate history and trial? Or is it the story of the child raised in modest beginnings and taught to fear an unforgiving God who built a hell just to punish the ambitious, the vain, and the dishonest for eternity? Is the moral here that one should pay more attention to accounting practices or is it the inevitability of the fall of a man who turned his back on the lessons learned in poverty and humility and carved out a life of riches, power, and fame—only to lose it all in the end? We think we can guess your answer.

The facts of the Enron case are a statement of what was "true" for one company. The Ken Lay story embodies a "truth" that contains a message for everyone in business that transcends the facts of his life and even his specific circumstances. Finally, the fall of Ken Lay is more compelling than the fall of Enron because it echoes stories we are already so familiar with.

In many ways, Lay's life parallels the classical Greek myth of Icarus, whose father, Daedelus, built a pair of workable wings from wax and wood for his son, but warned him not to fly too high. Icarus, ignoring his father's warnings, flew too close to the sun. The wax holding his wings together melted, and the prideful Icarus fell from the skies and died. The story has been told over and over again. Mary Shelley's 1816 story of Victor Frankenstein is another variation on the theme: The brilliant scientist, blinded by his ambition and the desire to master over the forces of nature, creates a monster who takes on an uncontrollable life of his own, ultimately destroying everything his creator loves.

The Use of Story as Positioning Statement

At the funeral service for Lay, held in Houston's First United Methodist Church on July 12, 2006, Reverend Dr. Bill Lawson invoked other stories to suggest that Ken Lay had been falsely accused. Lawson compared Lay to Dr. Martin Luther King, Jr., and Jesus Christ, providing a more-or-less effective example of how to use familiar stories to tell your story. The implication was clear—Ken Lay was a good man, possibly a great man, misunderstood by the society at large, vilified for crimes of which he was not guilty, and who was martyred and will eventually be not just redeemed but lionized.

The Mad Scientist in the Laundry Room

The distinction between *truth* and *true* is also critical in marketing, an arena where the *true* seems to be sacrificed in the name of *truth* on a daily basis.

It may be *true*, for instance, that based on objective chemical analysis, a Procter & Gamble research scientist sitting in his or her laboratory in Cincinnati may be able to use spectrographic analysis to demonstrate that Tide does, in fact, clean your laundry better than other liquid detergents. But we don't know of any laundry rooms that come equipped with either scientists or spectrographs, so most laundry doers make their soap purchases based on their truth, often expressed something like this: "My clothes are cleaner when I add Oxyclean to the wash water."

Is it true? As any good brander or marketer will tell you, that's not really the question.

When it's done well, storytelling—especially corporate storytelling—is an exercise in conveying truth statements rather than true statements. It's a way of positioning your company and its offerings against the market, one hopes not just for today but for decades to come. The best corporate stories are those that make sense no matter when they are told.

Paris Hilton, Jack Kerouac, Jason and Achilles

Truth statements achieve their timeless quality because they can be—and are—verified by personal experience throughout history and reinforced by both historical and popular culture. Each generation discovers the *truth* stories for themselves. Jason's search for the Golden Fleece is Jack Kerouac's *On the Road.* Achilles is the original "Rebel Without a Cause." Paris Hilton is a modern, female Narcissus, apparently endlessly fascinated by her own image.

True stories, on the other hand, are verified by contemporary observational methods and reinforced by condition. History teaches us that this kind of observation is, at best, perishable. It was *true,* for example, that the U.S.S. Maine was sunk by the Spanish, prompting the Spanish-American War, until it was discovered that the ship was really sunk by the U.S. Navy. It was equally true that Iraq had weapons of mass destruction until we invaded and found out they didn't exist. Events may be written by reporters on the scene, but history is written by the victors and amended—usually more than once—over time. The *truth* is constant, eternal, and immutable, whereas our idea of what is *true* is evolving and fluid.

21

Paradoxically, *truth* statements are objective—every element can be verified. Perhaps because of their lack of historicity, *true* statements tend to be subjective. They report what was apparently true as seen at the time.

Other critical differences distinguish what is *truth* from what is *true*. Truth statements are timeless (or more correctly, transcend time), whereas true statements reflect immediate circumstances. It was *true*, for example, that Enron was hailed as a model for future commerce. However, the *truth* is, it will serve the ages as a model of corruption.

As previously noted, *truth* statements are verified by historical experience and reinforced by culture, whereas *true* statements are verified by contemporary observation methods reinforced by consensus. *True* statements tolerate anomalies and even paradoxes, whereas *truth* statements are expressed in absolutes and tolerate no exception. If you're trying to make your sales numbers at the end of a quarter, for example, it might be functionally *true* that certain pricing models can be temporarily suspended, but the *truth* is that corporate policy can never be challenged or circumvented.

Importantly for corporate storytellers, *true* statements are defined by the context of their time, whereas *truth* statements define context. As discussed later, this ability to define context is becoming more and more critical to businesses each and every day. Later in this book, we return to the topic of context and what we call its abolition.

Other critical differences distinguish *true* from *truth*. Audiences—whether your external customers or your own employees—experience the *true* on a primarily intellectual level. They weigh product claims. They examine new changes in HR policy to see whether they've gained or lost. When a great storyteller presents a *truth*, however, the audience experiences it on a variety of levels—intellectual, emotional, spiritual (and, more often than not, a combination of all three).

What's *true* is generally expressed as data points, but the *truth* always comes in the form of a story. *True* statements are ends in themselves and can be tested. Truth stories, on the other hand, require an act of faith to believe and convey some meta-principle.

Throughout human history, storytelling has been used to communicate the most sacred *truths* of the collective human experience. Effective business communication, on the other hand, is traditionally viewed as the simple, direct, and timely transmission of relevant *true* statements.

To become an effective corporate storyteller, you must understand that your job is always to build the *truth*—of your company, of your brands, of your history, and of your values.

We spend the majority of this book examining the direct application of storytelling to business. First, however, it's important to take a look at the larger role myths, stories, and storytelling have played—and continue to play—in the daily lives of individuals and societies.

1976

"*Daddy, where did people come from?*" the four-year-old asked his father.

"So many questions," his father laughed. "Well, I don't know about all people, but our family is Irish, from a place called County Clare."

"How come our family left County Clare?" the boy asked, knowing his dad, the smartest dad in the whole wide world, would know the answer.

"People came to America for all kinds of reasons," his father told him. "They wanted freedom to go to whatever church they wanted."

"You mean like St. Peter's," the boy interrupted, happy to add a fact to the discussion he had launched.

"Exactly like St. Peter's," said his dad, handing him a dish of vanilla ice cream with more chocolate sauce than Mom ever gave him. "You see, our family was Catholic, like we are today, and the British people, who ran Ireland in those days, went to Protestant churches like St. Andrew's Episcopal down the street or Redeemer Lutheran, the church that's next to the park."

"But you still didn't tell me why they left their home," protested the little boy, guiltily entertaining the possibility that maybe his dad didn't know everything after all.

"I told you, son," his father said, a touch too sternly. "Our family wanted their freedom to live anyway they wanted. Besides, they were very hungry and very, very sad."

The little boy knew that if you got too hungry it could make you sad, especially if you were hungry for ice cream, but he was confused. "How come our family just didn't go to the supermarket and buy some food?" he asked.

"Well, for one thing, in those days there were no supermarkets, or jobs, or money. The British people ran things, and they were very, very hard on the Irish," his father told him. "So your great-grandfather Murphy came to Boston, where he opened a real Irish bar. Your grandpa was born here, and he went away in a big war called World War II and fought on the same side as the British."

"I bet that made his dad angry," said the boy.

"Not really," said his father, "because he was fighting for America, not England." The boy was confused but didn't interrupt. "I was born right after that war, and 24 years later you came along."

"We've always been proud of our roots," his father went on, even though the little boy couldn't remember asking a question. "And our family has never forgotten how our forefathers battled for their freedom. In Europe, you did what the government told you, but here we chose our own leaders. So when somebody tries to tell you what to believe, you tell them you can make up your own mind. You remember the lessons of our family and stay true to them, and you'll never have to leave your home, because you'll be happy."

The boy figured his dad had finally finished. "Can I have some more ice cream with our secret extra sauce?" he asked.

2006

"As most of you know, *Murphware* was created in 1999, right at the mid-point of the Internet bubble when Technomurph, the company my dad founded in the late 1970s, staged what's been correctly referred to as the friendliest friendly takeover in history—the acquisition of Wowieware, which John Wowitcz had established in 1989," Patrick Murphy, Jr., told the company's 2006 "freshman team."

"My dad and John Wowitcz were bound together by a common, passionate, visionary belief—the belief that because software is coded like DNA, it can replicate itself and can, and does, evolve over time—it represents a form of life, maybe the forerunner of an entire silicon-based universe. As many of you know, my father staked his personal and professional reputation on the principle that the quest for freedom is the organizing principle of all life. I guess you could say he 'grokked' Linux when Linux wasn't even cool. That belief, and the corporate culture that grew around it, is what separated, and still separates, us from the Oracles, the Microsofts, and others who saw, and still see, growth almost exclusively in terms of wealth and power. That's why today, at Murphware, our guiding standard is the one first, and best, articulated by John and my dad back in 1999: 'We shall never place profits over principles.' After all, it's immoral to limit a civilization's growth—and that's what the silicon ecology is, a civilization—in the name of patent protection, proprietary standards, or pure profit. Sure, we're as anxious for margin as the next guy, but we're not willing to put a price tag on freedom to get an edge in the market."

It was a story Murphware veterans had heard over and over again and a story Patrick Murphy never tired of telling. The story served several functions, not the least of which was to separate software "top guns" anxious to advance their career from the kind of dedicated team members Murphy needed to fulfill the vision his father shared with John Wowitcz. In the highly competitive software industry, it was tough to find people who weren't looking to re-create the financial magic that had existed before the bubble burst. Murphware was staffed by people who took a different tact, believing in developing software that worked right and could "learn" and "grow," customizing itself uniquely to every user's application.

"We're never going to be as big as the big guys," Murphy continued. "If you want to make your first $10 million before you're 30, this is probably not the right company for you. If we're right, one day our systems will drive everything. For those of you who stay, I can promise you personal as well as financial rewards. Those who leave, leave with my blessing and a warning that happiness isn't always found in a larger paycheck. Our work here isn't about code—it's about freedom and growth, for you and the software you design, and about your right to pursue happiness along with a career." As he hoped, the applause, tentative at first, grew in volume and confidence. A good story got them every time.

Chapter 3

THE 10 FUNCTIONS OF STORYTELLING

S torytelling is both a simple and complex activity.

Storytelling Lesson Number Two:
In the End, Storytelling Comes Down to
Two Things: Connection and Engagement.

Whether it's a shaman relaying his vision around a sacred fire, a tribal elder handing down his people's oral history, or a marketer pushing his or her newest line extension or service, it all comes down to these two fundamental elements.

The first task of any storyteller is to make a connection with the audience. Success and failure are defined early in the game. Lose the audience, and it doesn't really matter how important your story is. Think about the difference between Al Gore, former vice president and presidential candidate, versus Al Gore, promoter extraordinaire of *An Inconvenient Truth* (both the book and the movie) and pitchman for both global warming and a kinder, gentler, more ecologically attuned Democratic Party. The former was terminally stiff, the latter, almost charming (for a guy who is essentially still pretty stiff). We're not sure which got more attention when *An Inconvenient Truth* came out—global warming (its principle topic) or the fact that Gore had somehow found a way to soften his personal image and had suddenly become, if not laid back, at least far more accessible and "human." The new Al Gore is a guy you could connect with, kind of like the guy who defeated him in his presidential race in 2004. He is, in fact, the kind of guy who could tell you a story you might want to listen to.

Once a storyteller has connected with the audience, his or her next job is to engage them. We're defining *engagement* as the ability to build a connection and form a meaningful, sustainable relationship—generally, a relationship with strong emotional underpinnings. It's at the point of engagement that the audience becomes part of the story.

We don't want to rehash any of the well-honed discussions of so-called "cult brands," such as Krispy Kreme or Harley-Davidson, but the fact that some people will tattoo a brand name on their arms, chest, back, and even their face shows you how engaged with your story some customers can become. The same level of engagement is illustrated in reverse by boycotts, protests, and websites criticizing companies or their products. When people take time out of their lives to try to destroy your brand, product, or company, they are clearly engaged, albeit in a negative way.

Tell a good story, and you create a success. Tell a great story, and you can create a movement. Wrap a great story around an iconic symbol, and you can sometimes create an industry. When Michael Mann premiered *Miami Vice* on television on September 16, 1984, he launched more than a wave of chronic pastel abuse in America. Sure, even Kmart was selling faux-Armani (or to be more correct, cheap cotton "sport coats" the thickness of a work shirt dyed colors not found in nature), but the *Miami Vice* magic didn't stop with fashion faux pas.

Suddenly, every middle-aged, middle-class regular guy wearing a pastel Hanes T-shirt thought of himself as a hip, glamorous, danger-loving denizen of South Beach. It's easy to dismiss this kind of behavior as faddish or trendy, but that would be missing the point. Mann's Crockett and Tubbs characters (resurrected—at least in name—on the "big screen" in 2006 by Jamie Fox and Colin Farrell) weren't just television characters. They were the reincarnations of an iconic figure, the hero who bends, and sometimes breaks, the letter of the law to enforce its spirit. The wardrobe was different, but it was Robin Hood all over again. We respond to icons because sometimes they tell us a story without words. There's a reason Madonna, Gwen Stefani, and Christina Aguilera have all adopted a Marilyn Monroe-like persona at different points in their careers. They don't have to tell us the story, just remind us about it.

The power of remembrance is also the reason why telling familiar stories almost always conjures up a very specific preconditioned image or response in the mind of an audience.

Myth making and storytelling are universal elements present in all human societies, from the most primitive to the most advanced. The telling, preserving, and transmission of sacred stories—or more appropriately, stories sacred to a culture—define the human experience in far more robust ways than the use of an opposable thumb or the ironically mythical belief that man is the only animal to use tools.

Throughout the course of human history, stories have been used for every imaginable social function, from framing the social order and law, inspiring the creative, fueling the romantic, to justifying wars and explaining away unpopular peaces. For our analysis, we've focused on 10 discrete common, historical uses and functions of myths, stories, legends, and other lore. Master these 10 elements, and you're well on your way to becoming an effective corporate storyteller.

1. Explain Origins

The story of "the beginning" is the primal story. Every culture produces at least one origin myth or story. Across all times and cultures, these stories and myths have been used to answer humanity's most basic questions: Who am I? Where did I come from? Why am I here? What is my purpose? What happens after I die? Origin stories span the globe from the central Australian Arrernte myth of the Numbakulla brothers molding humanity from life forces trapped in the mud to the Judeo-Christian story of Genesis where Yahweh performs the same trick as a solo act. Origin stories are the critical foundation stones of all mythologies and cultures.

What does your corporate origin story say about where you came from, who you are, and where you are going? Consider a very top-line view of a couple of corporate origin stories, in this case, Wal-Mart and Apple. Wal-Mart's origin story goes back to Sam Walton, a modest man in a modest town providing good value to his modest neighbors. The origins of Apple, on the other hand, lead us back to Steve Jobs, the half-mad, half-visionary, always ephemeral technological boy genius. It's not hard to understand why the Wal-Mart story yields a company based on low prices for working folks, whereas the Apple origins result in a company that brought us the Mac and the iPod.

2. Define Individual and Group Identity

Once the basic existential questions have been addressed by an origin story, there's a need for a second set of stories. These tales begin to describe the relationship of the self to the other and, by extension, to all others. Often these stories are used to explain alliances or justify wars. They become the foundation of the traditional wisdom, or lore, of a people. Over time, elements of this traditional wisdom find their way into a people's formal history, language, culture, customs, and laws.

In business today, the spirit of this body of lore is found in the notion of the dedicated corporate team—a tribe within the corporate tribe, if you will. It's often used to color the story of battles for market share. It is the story of the Procter & Gamble tribe against the Unilever tribe; of the American "Big Three" versus the Japanese automakers; of Linux versus Microsoft; of Virgin, Southwest, Ryan

Air, and other low-cost air carriers against United, British Airways, Northwest, and Delta; and of Kodak battling Fuji.

Defining group or individual identity can also be an exercise in simple-order branding. "We're the good hands people" both serves as a definition of group identity for Allstate agents and as a brand promise for the company's customers. "At G.E. we bring good things to life" serves as a brand position statement and a statement of corporate ethos.

3. *Communicate Tradition and Delineate Taboo*

The need for an easily communicated, commonly accepted vehicle to explain social relationships and proper behavior has been present since the first group of cavemen warily decided to share a fire. They appear over and over again, from stories told in the Middle East to justify the Hebrew, and later Muslim, ban on eating pork to the early days of Silicon Valley, where they were used to describe the ostensibly de-hierarchalized Information Age workplace. It is why an extra plate is set at Passover ceremonies and why, at one time, all IBMers appeared to dress in the same uniform, built around a crisply pressed white shirt.

Establishing corporate traditions and delineating taboo behaviors are obvious tools for reinforcing group identity. For years, Ukrop's supermarkets in the Tidewater area of Northern Virginia have not sold beer—proving they are part of the community by embracing some community members' taboos against drinking. The no-beer policy links the stories of the supermarket company and the community it serves.

4. *Simplify and Provide Perspective; Reduce Complex Problems to a Series of Easily Digested Principles*

Almost all the topics addressed by classical stories tend to fall into the realm of the "meta-question." Myths in particular convert intricate themes into simple, universally accessible stories—

whether it's the ancient Aztec doctrine of the Five Suns or the San myths of the Southern Kalahari Bushmen, both of which explain how the universe and our world came to be, or the Sanskrit tales of the Ramayana, or the Hebrew Old Testament tales that describe the battles of good and evil.

But there are much more accessible corporate versions of the same technique. Consider the reductionist appeal of a phrase like "At Ford, quality is Job One." It's a sentence that tells a story, a story that transcends and eliminates the need for a complex discussion of plant capacity, engine size, vehicle safety, fuel economy, and value for money. Perhaps the classic one-line story belongs to Avis: "We try harder."

5. Illustrate the Natural Order of Things

Understanding where you are on the food chain is as critical in society as it is in business. This might explain why every pantheon of gods ever memorialized in fable comes neatly arranged in a nice hierarchal package. From Mt. Olympus to the Vedas, the pecking order is as crystal clear as the reasons behind it, typically having something to do with a divine version of seniority.

In the business world, we use a pictograph, a story in symbols—in this case, the organization chart—to illustrate the great corporate chain of being. The organizational chart not only tells us who is subordinate to whom, but it also sketches out the rationalization for the hierarchy. Department A reports to Department B, which in turns reports to Division X. First you find yourself, and then you find where you stand in relation to the whole.

6. Concisely Communicate Complex History

In their book, *When They Severed Earth from Sky: How the Human Mind Shapes Myth*, Elizabeth Wayland Barber and Paul T. Barber argue that preliterate societies like the Klamath tribe used myth to transmit historical information about real events such as the volcanic creation of Oregon's Crater Lake. The story version of fact is simply easier to remember and retell, eliminating any and all needless detail or unknown or contradictory elements. No consumer really wants to understand the chemistry and engineering of bathroom tissue. We're sure there are lots of scientific reasons why Charmin feels softer than its competitors. All that complexity would be lost if it weren't for the story of Mr. Whipple, the poor soul whose job it is to keep people from yielding to the temptation to squeeze the Charmin.

7. Communicate Moral and Ethical Positions and the Transference and Preservation of Values

The use of stories to reinforce values and behavior deemed critical to a tribe's or society's survival is easily documented. This kind of story, like the communication of complex history, reduces all extraneous elements to more profoundly make a point. Starbucks is a master of storming the moral high ground. Whether it's the commitment to fair trade coffee, the acquisition of Ethos water and the pledge to donate a portion of all sales to making potable water available to everyone on Earth, or giving away used coffee grounds for garden compost, Starbucks uses the stories of its charitable activity to tell its corporate story.

8. Illustrate Relationships to, and with, Authority

Think of these stories as variations on the Order of Things tales—only with far more dramatic punch lines. The Greek myths are particularly good at describing in uniquely gruesome detail the fate of those who argue with the boss or offend him in some manner. Ixion, for example, who killed his future father-in-law and tried to steal away with Zeus' wife, was stretched out for eternity on a wheel of fire. Sisyphus, who stole his brother's throne and gave away some of Zeus' secrets, ended up endlessly pushing a huge boulder uphill only to have it roll down every time he reached the summit. Tantalus decided to see exactly how powerful the gods were by feeding them the flesh of his own son. He spent eternity starving and being driven mad by thirst, standing in a pool of water that receded away from him every time he bent over to get a drink, while the world's most desirable fruit hung just inches from his reach. Well, you get the idea. The Greeks weren't big on defiance.

Neither are corporations, of course, which is why the fate of whistle blowers is spoken of only in whispers and why the move of an executive to a competitor is cast in the worst possible language. Oddly enough, one of the most common examples of creative storytelling surrounds how companies explain the sudden departure of key executives. They're never fired for cause, or just quit, or have a nervous breakdown. Instead, they leave "to pursue personal interests" or to "spend more time with their family."

9. Describe Appropriate Responses to Life or Model Behaviors

The stories of Adam and Eve and the Buddha both illustrate how the individuals discover themselves and become conscious after they leave home. The nature of love and fidelity is told in the story of Odysseus. The story of King Midas tells us what befalls those who let their appetites take precedence over reason. We could go on almost forever here because every myth has something to say about how life is—or should be—lived.

Years ago, the Pinkerton Detective Agency used to lure new recruits with stories of Pinkerton agents who had been martyred in service to the company. We wonder how effective these stories of very heroic—and very dead—agents were as a recruitment device, but they serve as an excellent example of this function of storytelling.

10. *Define Reward and Detail the Paths to Salvation and Damnation*

This final principle lies at the heart of the story of Lancelot's search for the Holy Grail and stories such as Dr. Faustus, Mary Shelley's Frankenstein, Robert Louis Stevenson's Dr. Jekyll and Mr. Hyde, the blues legends of Robert Johnson selling his soul to the devil at the crossroads of Highway 61 in Mississippi, and most recently the six-movie saga of the rise, fall, and eventual redemption of Darth Vader.

The bottom line—stories are all about connectivity. They trace the connections of people with each other and their society; organize their past, present, and future into a single continuum; help explain both the physical and metaphysical universes; and demonstrate correct and perilous moral and ethical behaviors, often with tales of rewards and punishments.

In Silicon Valley's boom times, the air was thick with stories of instant multimillionaires and Microsoft employees who apocryphally "called in rich" and quit working. In those pre-bust days, the road to secular salvation was clear: Have a great idea, find a financial angel, get your first run of capital, and don't burn completely through it until your second-round financing is in place.

Today's boardrooms dance to their own peculiar rhythms because any number of CEOs have listened too long to the "CEO story" that says the best way to manage is to drive shareholder value at any cost, cash in your options, and get out—all in 18 to 36 months. Are these stories true? We guess that in the case of the CEO story, the sad answer is yes. For other stories, it all depends on context, the subject of Chapter 4, "The Abolition of Context."

Mr. Black and Mr. White had a problem, and a fairly serious problem it was.

They had, it appeared—quite independently of each other of course—safely fallen asleep in their own cozy beds and somehow woken up—apparently simultaneously—in the same room. It was in every conventional sense of the term quite an ordinary room, exceedingly unremarkable in all aspects, you might say. All the room contained—besides them—was a single sheet of paper carrying this rather enigmatic sentence: *Agree on where you are and how you got here, and you'll be free.*

"Well, that seems simple enough," said Mr. White.

"I'm not so sure," countered Mr. Black.

"Well, obviously we're in a room," said Mr. White. "We could, of course, pace it off, so as to make the description a bit more—er—official-like."

"I'm not sure who you are, or if it's even within the seemingly limited capacity of your nature, but try not to be such a simpleton," snorted Mr. Black. "That's clearly too obvious an answer. Of course, this is a room and, of course, we could define its dimensions—more or less accurately since we don't have any measuring devices—but I don't think that's what the question means at all."

"Perhaps you're right," responded Mr. White, more cordially than he, in fact, felt. As a general rule, Mr. White was slow to anger, but there was something about his current circumstances and his uninvited companion's presumptuous and hostile attitude that mitigated his normal rather sunny view of the world. "But, still, if we are to get out of here, we have to able to agree to the things we can see. This is, without question, a room."

"Well, just suppose it isn't really a room at all," shot back Mr. Black. "Suppose it's really a box with cleverly concealed seams so that it looks like a room?"

"Maybe we're inside a large rectangular egg, laid by some prehistoric bird," said Mr. White, exasperated with his companion's obduracy.

"Quite so," said a suddenly reflective Mr. Black. "Perhaps you have something there. Not the prehistoric bird part, of course, but suppose we've been seized by the government, and this is some kind of top-secret military device, or some kind of test? If that's the case, they'll never let us out of here alive, or if they do, they'll have to kill us."

"Where do you get such insane thinking?" asked Mr. White, himself the most grounded of grounded souls. "We're clearly in some room. That much is obvious enough. Why we're here, how we got here, and who arranged for us to be here are more of a mystery. But if whoever put us here had meant us any real harm, they could have easily dispatched us in our sleep."

"Aren't you on the Internet?" hissed Mr. Black, retreating incredulously into a corner. "Everything is out there. You just have to know where to look. They're clever, all right. I'll grant you that. But even they can't hide forever. Besides, don't you see that the where, why, how, and who are really the same questions?"

"You, sir, are a ranting paranoiac," said Mr. White.

Suddenly it occurred to him there was nothing connecting him to Mr. Black. They had no previous relationship and worse, given the differences in their personalities and world views, they had nothing in common but proximity and the fact that a person or persons unknown had placed them in the same room, or box, or whatever it was. That person or persons seemed to believe they belonged together—constituting a set one might say—but from Mr. White's point of view, his unwanted companion was as different a creature as it had ever been his displeasure to meet.

Still, they had to find some common ground. If not, they would be trapped together in this otherwise unremarkable room until the end of their days. And when would those days come? A cold chill gripped Mr. White like an invisible steel claw tightly squeezing his intestines. He had no relationship with the people who were apparently treating him as a captive and trying, albeit on the most enigmatic of levels, to communicate with him. Mr. Black was clearly going to be no help in successfully answering his unseen captor's communication.

Across the room, Mr. Black viewed Mr. White with mounting suspicion. Why was he so apparently unruffled by their current shared circumstance? he wondered. Maybe he was a spy, a plant, one of them. Well, he'd show them all! No matter how Mr. White suggested they solve their puzzle, he would take the other side. Frustrate them. Wear them down. They'd see they shouldn't have bothered with someone as informed, as aware, as he was.

When it comes to communicating with a stranger, nothing, it seems, is ever Black or White, at least not at the same time.

Chapter 4

THE ABOLITION OF CONTEXT

The ability to communicate a commonly understood context is the bedrock of effective storytelling. But, as you are about to see, creating a fictional context is much easier than leveraging a cohesive social context—the kind of context you need to make storytelling work for business.

It Was a Dark and Stormy Night (or Was It?)

Read the following sentences carefully: The fog grew denser and more insistent with each hesitant step she took. It seemed to her to be a living thing, tentatively reaching out to touch her and quickly retracting into itself, then caressing her more insistently, clinging to her legs, inching steadily up her torso. Now the fog was almost taunting her, threatening to envelop and swallow her whole. The wind continued to pick up, and what, just a few moments ago, had been scattered drops of soft cool rain now felt like hundreds of slivers of ice tearing across the exposed flesh of her face. She began to smell her own fear, an acrid, sour smell that had followed her like a shadow all her life. She wanted to turn and run, away from the darkness, away from the fog, away from the sting of the rain, and most of all, away from herself and the smell of her own fear. But she had been running as long as she could remember, ever since something had happened, something she couldn't or refused to remember. So she plunged deeper into the shadows, deeper into the fog, anxious for it to be over at last.

If we've done a good job, you have a certain image in your mind. The context of that image will be more or less constant across readers. Many of you will see a woman walking alone through the night. There will be a howling wind, fierce rain, and an all-but-impenetrable fog. Likely, you might be imagining the woman near an ocean, possibly along a cliff. The air will be thick with fear and danger.

Because we gave you some of the details, you filled in the rest. We never said it was night. We never said the woman was alone or that she was by an ocean, let alone on a cliff. We're willing to bet that armed with a fairly consistent context, each of you has begun to tell yourself a slightly different story about who this woman is and what she's doing.

Some of you will see her as a teenager. Others will imagine a young newlywed, or perhaps a middle-age spinster—even an aging grandmother. She could be revisiting the scene of a long-forgotten childhood memory, or a place she had shared with a lover, or a place where she witnessed or caused an accident, or where she committed a crime or saw a crime be committed. She could be either unable or unwilling to recall what had happened, or she could begin to recall it with perfect clarity. She might be headed for a deep revelation, or final resolution, or personal peace, or danger, even death. She might be asleep and having an especially vivid dream or nightmare. She could be insane or experiencing a hallucination. Anything is possible, and having set the hook by painting a context, the storyteller is free to take the tale wherever he or she wants to take it—the audience's attention guaranteed, at least in the short run.

There are literally hundreds of scenarios that could—if we were to continue—unfold across the next few paragraphs and pages, clues that, when finally revealed, will tell us exactly why the woman was walking through the fog and what she hoped to find at its center. Give great storytellers an inch of context, and they can tell you miles of tales to fill the hours.

Common Understandings, Uncommon Stories

The 10 traditional functions of storytelling we discussed in Chapter 3 can be further reduced to a single, simple overriding principle: The function of a story is to provide a vehicle that allows the storyteller to communicate a set of images that can constitute an end in themselves or, in turn, communicate a specific point of view, moral principle, or other didactic device to his or her audience.

This ability to use words to drive to a calculated and preconsidered conclusion allows the storyteller a great deal of latitude. As you saw in Chapter 3, a simple story can help us understand who we are and where we came from, why we're here, and what is expected of us. Stories often describe—in very specific detail—the consequences of certain behaviors, both rewards and punishments. Told correctly, they offer us a way of relating to everything we experience, including other individuals. Great stories can make us laugh or cause us to cry. In short, they provide us a sense of continuity and order in what otherwise can be a fairly chaotic world.

In the same way that stories can build exponentially on a context, they are almost totally dependent on that context being collectively recognized by an audience. If an audience and a storyteller can't agree on a common basic framework for communication, it's all but impossible to tell a story that makes any sense.

Fictional Contexts Versus the Real World

Imagine trying to tell the story of the Three Little Pigs in a culture that sees swine as unclean at best or sinful at worst. Imagine reading a perfectly good story in Old English to a group of today's kindergartners. Even the most time-honored stories lose part of their power when they are taken out of a shared context. Think of Romeo and Juliet, one of the Western canon's most revered love stories. Now think of how differently that story is received by two audiences: the first a group of young suburban teenage Americans used to casual "hooking up" over a weekend; the second made up of traditional conservative Muslims from the Middle East, who understand exactly what it would mean (in the most literal terms) to defy their family's idea of who they should (or shouldn't) marry.

Our teenage audience might understand that parents are always a drag (and apparently always have been) and that true love is more important than keeping "the parentals" happy, but they might find killing yourself over it all just a tad over the top. The Middle Eastern audience, on the other hand, might be horrified at the idea of an illicit love affair but have no trouble seeing why life outside the narrow confines of cultural approval is impossible. The impact of the story, therefore, is completely dependent on the context in which the audience hears or views it.

This is not to say that stories aren't flexible enough to adapt to changing contexts and therefore capable of taking on new meanings over time.

The stories of Dr. Faust, who sold his soul for knowledge, and the legendary blues guitarist Robert Johnson, who allegedly sold his soul to the Devil at the crossroads of Highway 61 in the Mississippi Delta in exchange for the power to play guitar better than anyone ever had before, can have a meaning to an audience who doesn't believe in a literal Satan.

Such an audience might see the Devil as social conformity, or as a boss who asks you to bend the rules in order to advance, or entering into a bad marriage just to gain money or social position, or the personal dues you are asked to pay before you gain admission to a country club.

For Faust's original audience, God and Satan were physical beings, as real and tangible as a soul that could be lost, condemning a sinner to an eternity of suffering. And, for the African-American audiences Robert Johnson played before night after night, Satan was a real power broker of evil, a trickster who was always tempting those who strayed too far from the sanctified church. Given how church folk saw bluesmen, a pact with the Devil was as good an explanation as any for why Robert could make a guitar sound like nobody had ever made a guitar sound before.

The first English translation of *Faust*, in 1592, by a "P. F., Gent[leman]," was titled *The Historie of the damnable life, and deserved death of Doctor Iohn Faustus*, the "deserved death" a clear indication of how seriously the sixteenth century took even a story about trucking with the Devil. This wasn't some story about an idealist who had to swallow his or her personal morality or ethics to gain advancement in the corporate world. It was the story of a man so desperate for knowledge and the power it brings that he was willing to risk going to hell for eternity.

The Abolition of Context

In an earlier collaborative effort, *The Deviant's Advantage: How Fringe Ideas Create Mass Markets*, we suggested that the pace of change in contemporary society had resulted in what we call the Abolition of Context. We defined this state as the "—inability on the part of everyone and every business and society to find commonly agreed-upon reference points."[1] The Abolition of Context makes it difficult to make convincing brand or marketing claims. It is responsible in part for the decline of employer, employee, and brand loyalty, and it manifests itself in the challenges to corporate governance, from Enron to Global Crossing. In marketing terms, it can erode margins, market share, and advertising and merchandising effectiveness.

The root causes of the Abolition of Context are both myriad and diverse. They begin with the breakdown of the traditional social institutions like the neighborhood, the community, the church, the government, and the educational system, or at least our diminished trust in those institutions. These institutions used to reinforce each other, adding tiers of context on top of each other like the layers of an onion. The lessons learned in church were reinforced in the home. Secular versions of those principles were reinforced once again by community standards, neighborhood peer pressure, and in school. Of course, that was a time before the church-centered child-molestation scandals, Columbine, Monica Lewinski, invasion arguments based on the existence of weapons of mass destruction, two-income households, latchkey kids, and so on and so on.

Perhaps equally significant, it was a time before the Internet made it possible to be an expert on anything and impossible to have certitude about any individual authority. We used to know who "the world's leading authority" on a variety of topics was. Today, we have a hard time grasping the whole notion of authority. With all of cyberspace at our disposal, it seems impossible to believe that any one individual could possess enough information to be "the" definitive authority on anything. But what about just being an authority? You run into the same problem. Search the Internet long enough, and it becomes clear that having an unassailable fact-based opinion is almost impossible.

We live in an age where "Future Shock" has become déjà vu. In 1970, in his Introduction to *Future Shock*, Alvin Toffler wrote, "The acceleration of change in our time is, itself, an elemental force. This accelerative thrust has personal and psychological, as well as sociological, consequences."[2] He had no idea how right he was. The time it takes innovation (good and bad) to move from the society's fringe to its mainstream has compressed at a rate Toffler couldn't dream about, even on his most visionary day.[3] Things change so rapidly and so radically that the entire concept of a broad-based, widely agreed-upon social context is all but an anachronism.

Without a common context, it's hard to tell a convincing story. In Chapter 5, "Who Owns Your Brand?" we take a much more specific look at the consequences of the Abolition of Context on storytelling, especially when the storyteller is a large corporation.

Once upon a time, there lived a race of giants who towered over human beings like redwoods tower over mushrooms. Their immense height allowed the giants to share a unique and dizzying, if somewhat distorted, view of the earth. Sadly for the rest of creation, this perspective was theirs and theirs alone. Try as they might, all the giants could share with lesser life forms like humans were the products that emerged, fully formed, from their vision. The giants were known as brand marketers and managers, and they freely roamed the earth randomly dispensing their gifts—often in embarrassing overabundance—to anyone and everyone they met along their journeys.

"What's this?" the good, but simple folk asked the giants one day as they staggered under the weight of their latest unexpected gift.

"It's our Super Ultimate Formula Grease Relief," the giants answered, winking at themselves as they downed their third Chocolate Grey Goose Martini. "It replaces our Supreme Complete Grease Relief."

"But we thought Supreme Complete Grease Relief was the answer to all our grease buildup nightmares," the people cried out in despair and confusion. "You told us it would solve all our problems with personal, household, and environmental grease!"

"Obviously, you don't quite understand," the giants replied gently but firmly. "That was then, and this is now. Our vision is limitless, our inspiration eternal. New technologies are popping out of our R&D pipeline all the time. Concepts like 'best' and 'most effective' are only intellectual constructs after all—placeholders, if you will—until the verdicts of the new packaging focus groups come in. We can see you're confused and troubled. Relax. Trust us. We have only your best interests at heart. Turn on the television. Carefully watch our new ads for Super Ultimate Formula Grease Relief. Clip a few coupons that we've generously hidden in your mailbox and newspaper. Lighten up a little. Let us tell you a story that will explain everything."

And, in the fullness of time, the giants told the people the story of their latest product, over and over again until the people finally got it straight. Slowly, the people began to forget there had ever been a Supreme Complete Grease Relief. Soon the people were once again content that their grease problems were under control. After a while, full and complete order was restored. It was as if Super Ultimate Formula Grease Relief had always been with them. Supreme Complete Grease Relief was now less than a memory, the palest reflection of a shadow. Eventually, all was calm and right with the world. And it promised to stay that way, at least, of course, until the giants grew bored and blessed the people with another new product.

Chapter 5

WHO OWNS YOUR BRAND?

You Have to Let Go to Hold On

"Let go." That was the brand message Procter & Gamble CEO A. G. Lafley brought to the Association of National Advertisers' (ANA) 2006 annual conference. Lafley told the ANA audience that modern branders live in "a let-go world," where marketers are better served to "let go" of their brands and let consumer wants and needs drive brand strategy. He illustrated his point by showing a Pringles "commercial" created by a British teen and distributed on YouTube.[1]

Mildly damning the speech with faint praise on AdAge.com, *Advertising Age*'s Matthew Creamer noted, "The cry was somewhat unexpected coming from the chief of the consumer-goods marketer and advertising titan well known for carefully controlling perceptions of its sprawling collection of brands." Creamer concluded, "Mr. Lafley's address is probably best understood as a strong articulation of well-known marketing realities than anything groundbreaking.... Still, if P&G is starting to preach the gospel of letting go, even the world's more conservative marketers are bound to sit up and take notice."[2]

Not everyone believes in trusting the consumer. In a speech at the Idea Conference, Euro RSCG Worldwide CEO David Jones said, "We've got to stop thinking that consumer-generated content is an idea. It isn't. It is a phenomenon."[3] For the record, Jones also believes most of what appears on YouTube is "crap" and anti-brand.

With all due respect to everyone concerned, a critical point was universally missed both in the speech and in the coverage. It's impossible to let go of something that you're not holding on to in the first place. Consumers, not marketers, have become the de facto co-branders without portfolio of the twenty-first century. Put another way, the audience has become the storyteller. Increasingly, brands are being defined not by those who bring them to market but by the market itself. In Chapter 10, "Applied Storytelling 101: The Brand," we take a more in-depth look at how you can regain control of your brand story. For now, however, let's look at why brand storytelling isn't working as well as it once did.

The Uncooperative Co-Conspirators

Entire advertising-dependent industries—from consumer packaged goods manufacturers to the retailers who sell their products; to the American automotive industry, the dealers who sell its cars, and the after-market retailers who sell accessories and parts; to the media and entertainment industries—are discovering that the once terra firma of brand marketing is gradually being replaced by the commercial equivalent of quicksand.

There is no shortage of popular explanations for the erosion of brand loyalty. OgilvyOne Worldwide, for instance, blames the decrease on enhanced price promotion. "The pattern is clear," wrote Garth Halberg in an article posted to the company's website, "the greater the amount of price promotion in the market, the lower the perception of loyalty and the greater the difficulty of creating future loyal buyers."[4] The Ogilvy Loyalty Index research cited by Halberg gave consumers several ways to rate themselves, including "brand loyal," "price buyer," and "There are several different brands that I would choose between, regardless of the price"—a purchasing strategy the company calls a "repertoire" buying pattern. These repertoire buyers represent 51 percent of all fast-moving consumer goods buyers in America,

58 percent of all German consumers, and 44 percent of Indian consumers. A similar pattern is found for infrequently purchased categories and services.[5]

In fact "experts" can—and do—blame the decline of brands on almost anything and everything from Internet access to disgruntled brand consumers' opinions and pricing comparisons, to a jaded and cynical investigative media, to increases in product quality, to decreases in product cost.

We think the root cause of this decreasing brand loyalty and the growing inability to see differences between brands can be traced back to much simpler issues: the failure to tell a convincing story or, perhaps better said, the inability to tell a story convincingly and the inability to find and define, in a quite literal sense of the word, the audience.

The Little Bo Peeps Have Lost Their Sheep

Where have all the target markets gone? Well, some of them never existed in the first place, especially those defined by traditional demographics. Are Hispanics, for example, people with Spanish surnames? Or are they people who speak Spanish, so that second-, third-, and fourth-generation Mexican-Americans might not be "Hispanic" anymore? Here's how the U.S. government defines it: "**Hispanic Origin.** Persons of Hispanic origin were identified by a question that asked for self-identification of the person's origin or descent. Respondents were asked to select their origin (and the origin of other household members) from a 'flash card' listing ethnic origins. Persons of Hispanic origin, in particular, were those who indicated that their origin was Mexican, Puerto Rican, Cuban, Central or South American, or some other Hispanic origin. It should be noted that persons of Hispanic origin may be of any race."[6] Origin here being the key word. It's a definition so broad, so inclusive as to let in anyone who wants to belong through self-identification.

You run into the same problem with lots of other demographic labels, especially age, income (used as a correlative point to education), and even gender. People are forming voluntary tribes, self-defining cohorts that cruise comfortably below the radar of too many marketers. Don't believe us or think the point is stretched too far? Just cruise the Internet. That's where you'll find the mass of humanity at its digital and self-defining best.

Whatever theory you do (or don't) support, the bottom line for branders is the same. Every day, consumers are placing more and more demands on brands. And, every day, they grow more and more skeptical of at least individual brands' ability to successfully address those demands. Either branders are less and less capable of selling their stories or consumers are creating their own brand stories, or both phenomena are true. Look around. There are dozens of examples to choose from.

There are some instances of "happy accidents" where the loss of corporate control has actually helped a brand. Many of these have been examined in great length in other books and articles, so we'll just pick out two to illustrate our point.

Historically, Hormel thought of Spam as "tinned" potted pork. In recent years, the company has been smart enough to realize that a whole new generation of consumers see Spam as a "cool" food and have built a mini-cult around it celebrating the Spam experience in ways Hormel—and generations of older consumers—had never imagined. In the case of Spam, the product remained unchanged, but the story of the product was now one of fun-loving youthful rebellion.

For years, Harley-Davidson believed it was making high-performance motorcycles, until "Willy G" Davidson realized that Harley customers were customizing their bikes, transforming them into rolling icons of the "outlaw" or "free man" lifestyle. Eventually, Harley-Davidson successfully co-opted the myth of the outlaw bike club, reincarnating it as the corporately sponsored Harley Owners Group (H.O.G.), whose members sport its sanctioned colors and leatherwear and faithfully attend tribal gatherings. In Harley's case, not only was the story changed, the product itself was also significantly modified. Harley began to produce motorcycles that looked more like they looked after the customers chopped them—the perfect ride for the non-mechanically inclined dentist who wanted to live on the edge, but only on weekends.

Harley-Davidson and Hormel are two poster children for Lafley's "Let Go" philosophy. Both companies have profited by incorporating their customers' view of the brand into their branded product design and positioning and playing it back to the consumer, incrementally selling plenty of licensed goods in the process.

Now, let's look at the dark side of losing control of your story. When your audience begins to take control of your corporate or brand story, it starts to unravel and lose its hold. Your carefully crafted brand position is now 10 positions, or hundreds, or thousands, or tens of thousands. People begin to tell your story in the context of their experience and, for most brands, that means you've lost your "exclusive." This dilution of brand awareness, loyalty, and preference is supported by an increasing amount of research.

Instead of turning to a single brand or product for a definitive solution to a problem, consumers are now more likely to be loyal to a range of products or portfolio of acceptable brands.[7] Consumers aren't blindly buying brand claims and, as a consequence, brand stories are getting harder and harder to sell even in historically brand-conscious industries such as fashion. There are as many explanations for why consumers are shifting from loyalty to a single brand to tolerance of a portfolio of acceptable brands as there are marketing gurus pontificating on the topic.

In their study of over five years of more than 70,000 consumers in 12 nations, Fred Crawford and Ryan Mathews found an unarguable consumer preference for a "range of good" products versus a single best brand, which they believe is a response to frequent out-of-stocks on advertised items and an assumption by consumers that any product offered for sale ought to be relatively efficacious.[8] Lots of other people are reaching the same conclusion. Let's take a look at the high-technology industry.

Something's Rotten in Digiville (and Everywhere Else)

In 2004, Walker Information, which specializes in studying customer brand loyalty, found a decrease in loyalty among the traditionally ultra-brand-conscious consumers of high-technology products and services. As InfoWorld reported, "While the results reinforced the intuitive belief that loyal customers make for more successful companies, there was also an indication that the number of brand-loyal IT buyers is decreasing."[9] Not only did Walker Information find a 3 percent decrease in those identifying themselves as wanting, planning, and recommending a particular IT vendor, but 30 percent of respondents said they were "likely to continue doing business with the company, but not pleased with the relationship."

In other words—to paraphrase a well-known marketing slogan—they were buying the brand more, but enjoying it less. What Walker had tripped on was the tip of a very large (and growing) iceberg. Buyers of information technology aren't the only unsatisfied brand consumers out there. Consider what's happening in fashion, as we've noted, historically one of the most brand conscious of all industries.

In an article examining the results of the 2005 Brand Keys Customer Loyalty Index and its implications for the fashion industry, Valerie Seckler wrote, "Indeed, this year, Americans' expectations of apparel brands—including qualities such as style, fit and price—advanced 8 percent, while the success of the category's seven leading brands in satisfying those desires declined by 17 percent...The resulting difference of 25 percent [Authors' note: an actual difference of 25 percentage points, not 25 percent] means fashion ranks as the fourth least satisfying among 36 categories of goods and services, a group in which the most disappointing were long-distance phone service providers, where the gap extended to 30 percent."[10]

The Brand Keys research found that consumer expectations have increased in 35 categories, from financial institutions to fast food. As Kenneth Hein noted, "Across the full 222 brands, the average ability to keep up with consumer expectations fell 13.2 percent. Online book and music sites saw a 25 percent gap between rising expectations and their ability to keep up. Office copiers and car rental providers had a 24 percent gap while gasoline (23 percent) and airlines (21 percent) also struggled."[11]

Squirrels, Dogs, and Trees

Trying to sort out whether this is a cause or effect of the Abolition of Context that we discussed in the preceding chapter might be like trying to address the old pragmatist challenge to objective perception: If I watch a squirrel and a dog running around a tree, how do I know which one is chasing the other?

Truth Versus True: Round Two

Let's see how some of the ideas and tools we've introduced earlier in this book can be applied to this problem, starting with the notion of *truth* versus *true* discussed in Chapter 2, "Truth Stories Versus True Stories." As you'll see, companies can get into trouble by being on either side of the truth versus true line.

Coca-Cola is a company proud of the truth statement that when it comes to beverages at least, "Coke is it!" And, based on many of the truth criteria laid out in Chapter 2, it is. Coke's dominance of the beverage market goes back almost to the beginning of the modern soft drink industry. The history of the company, in many significant ways, defines the history of the industry.

Coke is so much a part of the American culture that its wintertime advertising campaign featuring the work of master illustrator Haddan Sundbom, first launched in 1931, cemented our modern vision of what Santa Claus looks like.[12] The notion of its supremacy was unchallenged (at least in its corporate headquarters in Atlanta) but, given the significant inroads of major competitors such as PepsiCo and upstarts such as Jones Soda, it increasingly requires an act of faith to believe. What is objectively true is that Coca-Cola has been late to market on the three most significant developments in modern beverage merchandising: bottled water, isotonic beverages, and bottled teas.

In the case of Coke, it would appear that the company's corporate belief in truth blinds it from addressing what's true. On the other hand, one could argue that without the truth, it would be in far worse shape, because to a large degree, it is everyone's shared vision of the Coke myth that allows it to be seen as a vital competitor rather than a company suffering from the effects of a succession of failed management visions. For Coke, the challenge will be to bridge the gap between the mythic truth and market truisms before it's too late.

In part, Coke is attempting to address the current competitive challenges by trying to resell its old corporate stories. Let's look at two examples.

The first example is more icon than actual story, although it's an icon of fabled proportions. The hoopskirt bottle—one of the most significant breakthroughs in the history of consumer packaged goods design—is now being modified into a can. The second appears in the form of television spots for Coke Zero that show a young man killed by a poison dart before he can share the "secret formula" with the audience before returning it to a vault. It's a 2006 version of the oldest of Coca-Cola's corporate stories, created when Ernest Woodruff, the Atlanta druggist who founded the company, figured out that having a secret formula was a great marketing gimmick.

The formula mystique is a story in itself. It began in 1925 when Woodruff retrieved the original formula from a New York City bank, where it had been languishing since being used to collateralize a sugar loan. The formula was then stashed in a safe deposit box in Atlanta's The Trust Company of Georgia. That same year, Woodruff upped the formula mystery ante by creating a policy that no Coke employee could see the formula without first obtaining the written permission of the board, and then only if the president, chairman, or corporate secretary were present. That's also when a policy was created saying that only two executives (whose identities were to remain anonymous) could know the policy at any given time.

Paradoxically, even though their identities aren't "public," company policy prohibited them from flying on the same plane, so a quick merge/purge of executive travel schedules might reveal who they were. So, the young man in today's television ads may know the secret formula, but as a variation on a famous jokeless punch line goes, if he tells you, they'll have to kill him. Of course, the ad only really makes sense if your memory stretches back to the 1920s.

Coke isn't the only company to resurrect an old story in an attempt to bolster sales and brand image.

General Motors' Buick Division spent $120 million in 2003 and an additional $57 million in the first half of 2004 trying to revise the story of Harley J. Earl, the father of modern automotive design, who was responsible for, among other things, the Corvette and the Firebird. Earl was convinced that automotive design could not only influence buying decisions but actually change the world and the way consumers thought about cars.

In Modes and Motors, a 1938 General Motors brochure, Earl wrote, "Out of the merger of art, science, and industry have come new techniques that have, within themselves, the ability to create an entirely new pattern and setting for the life of the world."[13] Earl was dead on in terms of his vision of the emergence of a whole new consumer context. Sadly, new car buyers didn't seem to understand what a guy who had retired before 1960 had to do with today's cars.

The truth of market supremacy or the myth of industry leadership has gotten any number of companies into trouble. What's good for General Motors is no longer good for the United States, despite the disturbing parallels between the eventual fate of GM's pension fund and Social Security.

The appeal of the story of the Crest kids and the ADA Seal of Approval didn't protect Procter & Gamble from market assaults by Colgate's Total and credibility attacks by Rembrandt and Tom's of Maine. The legend of Big Blue didn't stop Microsoft from pulling a fast one on IBM. In fact, it arguably helped Gates and company, who seemed to understand how to use IBM's corporate mythology against the company.

The point here is that in the absence of context, the lines separating what's true in a factual sense from contextual truth get hopelessly blurred. And when that lack of context is exacerbated by customers taking control of a brand's story, the results are tumultuous at best and disastrous at worst.

So, if the audience has really hijacked the story, and context is really being abolished, and the lines between the truth and what is true are less and less meaningful, how do companies, and individuals inside companies, reestablish a sense of identity? And how can you effectively communicate any sense of corporate or brand identity? Our answer—not too surprisingly—is through the application of classical myth making and storytelling.

"It Floats!"

In Chapter 3, "The 10 Functions of Storytelling," we looked at 10 functions of stories and storytelling. The first of these was to explain origins. Origins are critical to understand because the origin story often contains a key value that becomes enshrined in corporate identity. Andrew Carnegie's poor immigrant roots became a metaphor for the unlimited opportunity and power of the American experience, especially as that experience was embodied by U.S. Steel.

The official history of Ivory Soap stresses that, although floating soap was the result of an industrial accident, it was an accident that occurred "...after years of experimentation with various formulations...," resulting in the development of a soap formula "which was satisfactory in every respect."[14] Making an accident appear more important than the years of product development might set the wrong tone, especially for a company that prides itself on its ability to recite a litany of hard-science-based product breakthroughs.

While we're looking at P&G, let's examine the official explanation of the disappearance of the "Moon and Stars" logo.

The Moon and Stars image first began appearing on cases of the company's candles in the 1850s. By the 1860s, the logo could be seen on all the company's products. According to the company's website, in 1991, "The company introduced a new logo and wordmark to provide a more contemporary and consistent global look."[15] What isn't mentioned are the years of controversy and boycotts—real and threatened—by religious fundamentalists who insisted on believing that the logo was emblematic of the company's alleged association with the Devil.

Saying the origin of the new logo was in response to the verities of global commerce sets a much different tone than suggesting that the company may have caved under pressure from the lunatic fringe of the religious right.

Although the makers of Baileys Irish Cream make no attempt on their website to conceal that their product didn't debut until November 26, 1974, we're willing to believe that a good number of the consumers who are popping a mind-numbing 2,000 glasses of the product down their throats every minute believe that the original recipe was developed by sweet old Ma Bailey somewhere in the historical shadows of Bunratty Castle.[16] How disappointed would all those foster sons and daughters of Erin be to learn that the original inspiration for the drink was a very British home remedy for ulcers?

The point here is that origin stories help set the tone for a corporation's image. That explains why Sir Thomas Lipton's tea was consumed—and endorsed—by a generation whose grandchildren preferred Celestial Seasonings, which traces its origins back to Aspen, Colorado, in 1969, when Mo Siegel, a 19-year-old hippy, and his friend Wyck Hay wandered around the mountainside harvesting herbs.[17] In 1969, the story of a couple of hippies searching for ways to become closer to the earth and the Gaian world soul proved more compelling than the story of an authentically British tea.

Who Am I? Who We Are

Throughout time, one of the primary functions of stories has been to define individual and group identity, or in the business environment, corporate and brand identity.

Marshall McLuhan once observed, "Perhaps we tend to define myth in too literal a way, as something that can be verbalized, narrated, and written down. If we can regard all media as myths and the prolific source of many subordinate myths, why cannot we spot the mythic aspect of the current hula-hoop activity?"[18] Noting that 30 years before, children had viewed hoops as something to be rolled down roads and sidewalks rather than twirled around torsos, McLuhan said, "Here is a myth we are living." In McLuhan's expanded definition, the "myth" of spatial sense separated and defined generations.

Seem a tad too abstract? Apple used this principle to market the iPod, displacing the Discman as the primary weapon in the arsenal of the perpetually musically plugged in. What parent hasn't thrown up his or her hands after trying to communicate with a child whose personal communication ecology included an iPod, YouTube, MySpace, instant messaging, and cell phone texting, but not apparently the English language?

By defining a collective story or group myth—especially in the expanded McLuhan use of the term—corporations can draw distinct lines in the commercial sand between themselves and their competitors, definitions often adopted by both their employees and their customers.

IBM users "Think," whereas Apple users "Think Differently." In the early years, IBMers dressed like serious thinkers—white shirts, blue suits, and sensible ties. Apple staffers, on the other hand, prided themselves on the depth of their corporate T-shirt collections. IBM became the computer of the accountant. Apple was, and still is, the machine of choice for the artist.

Products often become the reification of the stories of their origin. "Made in Japan" used to be linguistic code for "terrible quality," whereas today "Made in Japan" is often a guarantor of product efficacy.

Anheuser-Busch recently aired an advertising campaign suggesting that their beer is better because it's made in America by Americans. Miller beer, the unspoken target of the campaign, also is made in the United States, we assume by Americans, but its corporate parent, SABMiller plc, is based in South Africa.

We're not positive how effective the Anheuser campaign was, or how seriously the Miller folks took it, but Miller's official online history does manage to pack eight references to the United States (or America) into its brief corporate history.[19]

A Hundred Thousand Commandments

The third function of storytelling is to communicate tradition and delineate taboo. With all due respect to people of faith, the clearest examples of this can be found in the business of organized religions. Religions have used taboo as an effective marketing tool forever. But taboos are, by their nature, negative motivators. So smart companies use myth stories to establish positive behaviors. Consider the "story" of unrelenting innovation, which has become the perceived tradition at 3M.

The company's official history, *A Century of Tradition: The 3M Story,* has chapter after chapter of bromide-laced tradition reinforcers.[20] A sample ought to suffice: Chapter 2, "3M Innovation—A Tolerance for Tinkerers"; Chapter 3, "3M

Innovation—How It Flourishes"; Chapter 4, "Ingenuity Leads to Breakthroughs"; and Chapter 5, "No One Stands Alone." You, and we're guessing every 3M employee, get the idea. The truth, of course, is a tad different. It took Post-it Notes from 1968 to 1981 to get real acceptance at 3M.[21]

Businesses that master this element of storytelling enjoy an inordinate marketing advantage, especially when they are associated with industries that people perceive as needlessly complex. Exhibit A: Saturn, the "different" car company. On its website, Saturn explains, "Saturn was created with one simple idea: to put people first. With the mission to create a different kind of car company—one dedicated to finding new ways for people to work together to design, build and sell cars—Saturn has earned a reputation for superior customer satisfaction."[22] There's no obvious reference to Saturn's parent, General Motors, which can't really share in the benefits of your average reductionist myth.

Despite some stumbles like the Gateway Country Stores, Gateway still tries to promulgate itself as a company based on and revering the same simple Midwestern values—honesty, trustworthiness, neighborly behavior, and so on—associated with its 1985 origins in an Iowa farmhouse.[23] Of course, the idea that cow print graphics can conceal a headquarters move to Irvine, California, doesn't really exemplify those values.

Let Me Tell You Where You Stand

Not all corporate stories are intended for external audiences. Many, in fact, are intended, formally or informally, to create and communicate a strong sense of internal order. Consider, for example, the myth John Teets created of the tough, super-testosteroned CEO who pumped iron only as a prelude to arm wrestling life to the ground.

Teets, who retired as Greyhound Corporation's chairman in 1997, became famous for saying, "Management's job is to see the company not as it is but as it can be." Teets was equally famous for his calculated portrayal of the CEO as alpha male. Facing a strike at Greyhound, Teets had a promotional film made showing him pumping iron. "I'm tough," Teets was once quoted as saying, "tough like leather, with just enough give to take a beating all day long and not shatter."[24] The Teets myth was communicated clearly to his subordinates. "He'd rather kick a door down than turn the handle," is an emblematic quote ascribed by *Fortune* to a company vice president and by MonteryHerald.com to Teets himself.[25]

Despite the ambiguous sourcing of the quote, Teets's sense of the leader's role in the corporate hierarchy is clear. "I think it's very simple," he told MontereyHerald.com, "leadership is by consent. People will consent to follow you if you take them where they can't go on their own." And how do you do that? Teets's answer to another interviewer was equally simple. "Sometimes," he said, "you just have to shoulder your way into a culture."[26]

Maybe it was a 1990s thing. It was, after all, the same era that produced the self-styled Chainsaw Al Dunlap, former CEO of Scott Paper and Sunbeam, who was famous for ruthlessly slashing operating costs. Dunlap once reinforced his image as "Rambo in pinstripes" by posing in Stallone-like attire for the cover of *USA Today*.

Internal audiences are just as likely—or perhaps more likely—as external audiences to "hear" your corporate story differently than you tell it. How many of us have had employees tell us about the sins and hypocrisy of their employers? We're willing to bet the answer is almost all of us.

Simplify. Simplify. Simplify

In storytelling, as in life, the KISS (Keep It Simple, Stupid) principle often applies. *Finnegans Wake* is a classic, but how many people do you know who have ever read—or understood—it? Simple stories can concisely communicate complicated histories. General Electric could get all caught up with the world of Thomas Edison. Instead, it expresses its rich and complex corporate history in simple terms: "Starting with the light bulb, innovation has been the foundation of our past and the key to our future."[27] You can't get much more concise than that and still be complete.

Letting the Audience Tell the Story

Storytelling can also communicate moral and ethical positions and preserve and transfer values. One proof point of effective storytelling is to see whether an entire audience has heard the same story and whether they can repeat it in their own context. A quick visit to McKesson Corporation's website (www.McKesson.com) offers an interesting demonstration of this point. In the "Corporate Culture" section, the text under the headline explains:

> Empowering healthcare is more than a tenet; it is the value we place on the work we do. Extending this empowerment begins with inspiring each of our valued employees, inside a place driven by friendly, people-focused teammates.... Best of all, whether it be a direct contribution or one shared collaboratively, each of our 24,000 teammates makes an impact.

> This unifying point of impact sends a clear signal to everyone—employees, customers, investors, and competitors alike—that McKesson is a company that measures its actions against a set of values shared by all. It's a source of inspiration driven by our mission to make a difference

in people's lives—the very mission guided by our ICARE Shared Principles:

- Integrity—doing what's right
- Customer-centered—we succeed when they succeed
- Accountability—taking personal responsibility
- Respect—treating people with dignity
- Excellence—insisting on quality

Now, that's a pretty good values statement, but what really brings it alive is that each of these five points is illustrated by a quote from a different rank-and-file McKesson employee under a section labeled "What does [the specific value] mean to you?"

Can't You Hear That Whistle Blowing?

Almost all myth cycles address the individual's relationship to authority. Sometimes in the business world it's hard to separate this application from several other storytelling functions, including establishing the natural order and transferring taboo. It might be helpful here to think about the collective myth of the corporate whistle blower. Some whistle blowers have survived their brush with authority and prospered. David Franklin, a scientist with Pfizer, won a $27 million settlement in a case in which he accused the pharmaceutical giant of off-marketing a drug for unapproved uses.[28] Sherron Watkins is another poster child for whistle blowing. She brought down Enron, was named one of *Time* magazine's "People of the Year," and has developed a lucrative consulting and public-speaking practice.

But most companies would rather their employees use Ed Bricker as their whistle-blowing model. In the 1980s, he went undercover for Congress to expose dangers in a nuclear power plant in Hanford, Washington. In 1994, Bricker won a whistle-blowing lawsuit against Westinghouse and Rockwell, but he only received $200,000. As the then 49-year-old Bricker told *USA Today*, "Where am I going to go? Who's going to hire me?"[29]

What's It All About?

Describing appropriate responses to life and modeling behaviors are also critical functions of any story. In corporate environments, this process begins with the interview and selection process. Respond correctly, and you move to the next level. Respond incorrectly—that is, in a culturally unacceptable manner—and you'll be politely shown the door. Most companies don't trust you to remember what you've demonstrated you've already learned. So new employees are handed fat handbooks outlining acceptable behaviors and are often assigned a mentor whose real job is to get them acculturated to the ways of the current tribe as soon as possible.

It has always struck us as a bit paradoxical how companies that are clearly so good at implementing this aspect of myth propagation often try to hide their success under a blanket of rhetoric about encouraging diversity and innovation. We've never sat in a single mission-critical meeting in which somebody didn't invoke their corporate mythology to negate an otherwise perfectly good idea. Think about it. How many times in your corporate career have you heard phrases like, "Well, you know we tried something like that (fill in the blank) years ago, and it just didn't work."

What's in It for Me?

The final function of stories we looked at in Chapter 3 had to do with defining reward and detailing the paths to salvation and damnation. Pick up any business magazine or scan the contents of the business section of your local Borders or Barnes & Noble store, and you'll be dumbstruck by the millions of words devoted to how to get to the top, explaining how one got to the top, or outlining behaviors that need to be avoided if you have any hope of getting to the top. Achieving corporate nirvana—the CEO's chair—is a matter of having perfectly balanced corporate karma.

If you're interested, there are plenty of gurus out there anxious to share the secrets of that balancing act for a paltry $29. In the end, the myth of success may be the story that compels people's most slavish if less-than-critical attention.

Oh sure, there are lots of folks who claim they knew John Abel, but if you ask me, it's like that movie *Citizen Kane.* After any great man dies, armies of people come out of the woodwork saying they were his friends, close acquaintances, or at the very least, always called him by his first name. Maybe they can tell you an amusing story—with themselves as the witty hero, of course—or point to a picture on their office wall as proof of a relationship, but in the end, none of them has a clue who the hell the "great man" really was.

Well, I knew him. Knew him when he was a kid. He wasn't likable then, and money didn't make him any more likable. He was a mean child and weak, the kind of kid who gets his lunch money taken away, or his clothes stripped off him at recess, or just plain gets punched out because he looks like he had it coming. In his case, he always had it coming. But John Abel wasn't your ordinary sissy kid. No sir. Even from the beginning, he kept a list of all the people who had ever hit him or hurt him in any way. He kept that list going his whole life, adding names whenever he felt a new slight, and only scratching names off when he felt "justice" had been done—which usually meant somebody had died.

But, like I said, I knew him before he was "John Abel, Business Titan" and well before there was an Abel Technologies. We met in middle school. I was big for my age and fast with my hands. What I wasn't good with was schoolwork. So we did a deal, maybe the first important deal in a career full of important deals. I'd protect little Johnny and, in my spare time, "punish" anyone dumb enough to find their way onto his list. In exchange, he saw to it my GPA soared from a solid D average to nearly straight A's. It was a marriage made in hell, which is what you get when you start dating the Devil, I guess.

Like lots of bad marriages, it turned out to be a lifetime commitment. Neither of us was happy with the other, but we never considered a divorce. I was comfortable—if you can call a lifetime of calculated and consistent humiliation comfort—and he...well, he never had to risk seeing what happened if his "pet bulldog" wasn't there for him.

You all know the story of the business. John started it in his grandparents' garage. He had to. His parents hated him, like almost everybody else. I had lost track of him after high school. He went to MIT, and I went, with a firm push from a judge, into the army. I re-upped after my first tour was over, and by then John had developed the first versions of his unhackable software. I left the army a little early following a small disagreement with a captain and met up with John when I drifted home. It was the same old story. He had a good idea, but all the bigger players were muscling him out of the industry. We ran into each other on the street and decided to reestablish our old arrangement.

I managed to persuade a couple of John's competitors to release their distributors from their exclusivity agreements, and the rest, as they say, is history. I don't know what John wanted; maybe he didn't either. But it seemed to me he was always struggling to be feared on his own terms, as a man, not as a businessman. He tried everything—personal trainers, kickboxing instructors, yoga. He never got there.

This search for self-confidence or whatever it was almost destroyed him. He focused so much on being the toughest business guy around that he started making enemies left and right. The business grew, but all of a sudden every software jock around the world wanted to hack the hack-proof system or develop a more competitive product or both. The distributors got a little tired of being beat up, too. Pretty soon the analysts were whispering about John being unstable and the company being just John in the end. The stock started to drop faster than an out-of-town conventioneer who's drinking in the wrong bar. Lots of the rats John had flogged nearly to death abandoned ship and went to other companies, taking some of John's secrets with them. I visited several of them to help them see the error of their ways, but there's only one of me, and people were starting to talk.

Just as it looked like John was about to lose it all, he pulled a fast one. For months he had locked himself in his office programming code in ways nobody ever thought of—even himself. When he came out, he was a changed guy. All that mattered to him was saving the business and shutting up the critics. I don't think even the money meant anything to him. It wasn't about little Johnny Abel versus the world anymore; it was just about Abel Technologies taking back the market. All the personal fear seemed to have been burned away like a meteor disintegrating when it re-enters the atmosphere. What was left was an even colder bastard than the one who had started the company in the first place.

Business is funny, though. Abel Technologies acquired or crushed its competitors and became the world's leading software solutions provider for governments, financial institutions, organized crime—anybody who wanted to make sure nobody could ever access their dirty little secrets. John's picture landed on all the covers, from *The Economist* to *Wired*, as technology's Comeback Kid. People were so afraid of him that he became the darling of capitalists everywhere.

Don't believe what you read in all the magazines about the late, great corporate philanthropist John Abel. The guy never gave more than he took, not since I met him back in middle school. Yeah, those guys might have pictures of John on their walls, but I've got all the scars.

Chapter 6

FIVE CRITICAL STORY THEMES

*"Storytelling reveals meaning without
committing the error of defining it."*
—Hannah Arendt

In the Beginning, There Were the Plots

We'll never know the first story, or the name of the first storyteller, or how many people he or she told the story to, or what it was about. It's possible, in fact, that the first story predates language, that it was traced with a stick in the mud or acted out rather than spoken. All we can know with any reasonable degree of certainty is that the story was one of humanity's earliest and most useful tools. Chipping stone allowed us to become better predators, harnessing fire allowed us to stay warm and safe, but stories let us remember the past, interpret the present, and dream about the future. The story is our link to ourselves, a transtemporal, transcultural, universal guide to what it means to be human.

When it comes to shaping your corporate story, you can relax a bit. Odds are "your" story was actually created a millennium or two or three ago. All you have to do is adapt a few new details to a time-honored plot. Almost everyone who has ever thought about plots seems to agree that there are a finite number of core story lines, subject to a near infinite number of variations. The problem is that nobody seems to agree what that finite number is.

The most draconian view of the number of story lines available to you was captured by Cecil Adams. "One school of thought," Adams wrote, "holds that all stories can be summed up as Exposition/Rising Action/Climax/Falling Action/Denouement or to simplify it even further, Stuff Happens, although even at this level of generality we seem to have left out Proust."[1]

Do We Hear More Than One?

Ronald Tobias, whom we'll revisit in a minute in greater detail, has argued that all plots can be reduced to two major categories, which he calls "plots of the body" and "plots of the mind."[2]

The same spirit of pigeonholing prompted William Foster-Harris to reduce his list of plots to three: happy ending, unhappy ending, and the "literary" plot.[3]

Jessamyn West, an Internet Public Library volunteer librarian, supplies us with a somewhat more useful list of seven basic plots or stories:[wo]man versus nature, [wo]man versus man, [wo]man versus the environment, [wo]man versus machines/technology, [wo]man versus the supernatural, [wo]man versus self, and [wo]man versus god/religion.[4]

Christopher Booker is another adherent of the seven-plot school. His candidates are "Overcoming the Monster," in which a hero struggles with the personification of evil, escapes death, and saves his or her community or the world from evil; "Rags to Riches," in which a poor character rises to great wealth or power; "The Quest," in which a hero starts out in search of a prize, enjoying fabulous adventures along the way; "Voyage and Return," in which our hero leaves his or her normal life, enters an alien realm, and returns safely home; "Comedy"; "Tragedy"; and "Rebirth." Oddly, after compiling his list of seven plots, Booker adds two more—"Rebellion" and "Mystery"—making his "list of seven" actually a list of nine.[5]

Perhaps realizing his list of two was less than fully utilitarian, Ronald Tobias provides us with an expanded list of 20 plots:

Quest, Adventure, Pursuit, Rescue, Escape, Revenge, the Riddle, Rivalry, Underdog, Temptation, Metamorphosis, Transformation, Maturation, Love, Forbidden Love, Sacrifice, Discovery, Wretched Excess, Ascension, and Descension.[6]

In 1921, Georges Polti published his list of 36 plots in *The Thirty-Six Dramatic Situations*.[7] His list contains the following plots: Supplication, Deliverance, Crime Pursued by Vengeance, Vengeance Taken for Kindred upon Kindred, Pursuit, Disaster, Falling Prey to the Cruelty of Misfortune, Revolt, Daring Enterprise, Abduction, the Enigma (temptation or riddle), Obtaining, Enmity of Kinsmen, Rivalry of Kinsmen, Murderous Adultery, Madness, Fatal Imprudence, Involuntary Crimes of Love (think Oedipus), Slaying of a Kinsman Unrecognized, Self-Sacrificing for an Ideal, Self-Sacrifice for Kindred, All Sacrificed for Passion, Necessity of Sacrificing Loved Ones, Rivalry of Superior and Inferior, Adultery, Crimes of Love, Discovery of the Dishonor of a Loved One, Obstacles of Love, an Enemy Loved, Ambition, Conflict with a God, Mistaken Jealousy, Erroneous Judgment, Remorse, Recovery of a Lost One, and Loss of Loved Ones. Of course, there are other plots that could be added to this list, such as Mistaken Identity.

You get the idea. The key point here is that regardless of how many story lines, or plots, or Ur-myth (the original, pure, pre-literary version of a myth or story) you believe exist, they can be fitted, or in some cases retrofitted, to explain almost anything.

The story of Prometheus defiantly challenging fate by stealing fire from the gods is the story of Walter Reuther fighting the forces of the Ford Motor Company's "Service Department" on May 26, 1937 at the (by now mythical in every important sense of the word) Battle of the Overpass in Dearborn, Michigan. It's also the story of Lance Armstrong overcoming cancer and self-doubt to win the Tour de France in 1999. In a peculiar way, it's also the story of Martha Stewart going to jail and emerging stronger than ever.

The story remains the same; only the names of the characters and the description of the background change. This ability to remain relevant across time is the real key to the power of story-telling. As Karen Anderson has noted:

> When Freud and Jung began to chart the modern quest for the soul, they instinctively turned to classical mythology to explain their insights, and gave the old myths a new interpretation.

> There was nothing new in this. There is never a single, orthodox version of a myth. As our circumstances change, we need to tell our stories differently in order to bring out their timeless truth.[8]

The trick, of course, given the Abolition of Context, is to find some point of reference to anchor the stories to. For most businesses, this requires the construction of a more complete context for a story. It is not enough to tell the story of a god today; you must first create a plausible picture of a heaven.

As we've just demonstrated with our cursory view of plot theory, tracking myths back to their seminal roots has been, and is, a cottage industry for artists, philosophers, writers, students of literary history, and more recently, psychologists, sociologists, and New Age therapists and business consultants. Most of these efforts focus on identifying the key mythic archetypes or meta-plots and then forcing them onto some preconceived mold to "explain" behavior.

Fortunately, trying to decide which ranks first, the Quest or the Resurrection, isn't our problem. To illustrate our point, we've selected six classic myth themes (story lines, if you prefer) that appear in every culture we can find. If they aren't universal, they're pretty close, and we think part of their global appeal lies in their ability to reduce some of the most critical issues in individual and—by extension—collective or institutional lives to a set of simple stories.

For the record, we aren't claiming these are the only story lines we could have looked at. They do, however, align with what we describe in Chapter 7, "Five Stages of Business Evolution," as five critical stages of business evolution and provide keys to successfully passing these personal and corporate hurdles.

The Hero's Quest

Let's begin with the first of our plot lines, the Hero's Quest. The story itself is one of the most familiar in all cultures: Heroes set off on quests that, if successful, will fulfill all their ambitions and cause them to realize their destinies. If the quests are unsuccessful, the price will be the heroes' lives or the lives of those the heroes love. In some cases, the stake is an immortal soul or an eternity of pain and suffering. Generally, if the heroes are successful, their quests serve a greater good—removing a curse, restoring prosperity to the land, driving out some evil force or forces, or bringing a gift to the community.

Here's how Joseph Campbell, perhaps America's greatest student of mythology, religion, and folk wisdom, described the Hero's Quest:

> A hero ventures forth from the world of common day into a region of supernatural wonder: fabulous forces are there encountered and a decisive victory is won: the hero comes back from his mysterious adventure with the power to bestow boons on his fellow man.[9]

Of course, the story takes many forms depending on the time and culture. Odysseus (Ulysses), the hero of the Trojan War, sought only to go home, but even that simple quest was made nearly impossible because he had angered the gods. Jason sought out the Golden Fleece. Goethe's Dr. Faust sold his soul as the price of his quest for hidden knowledge. On a more contemporary note, the 2007 release of *Ghost Rider*, the movie version of the story of the half-man, half-demon motorcycle-riding comic book hero, is the latest variation on an age-old theme.

The Hero's Quest takes as many forms as there are languages and cultures. Its lessons, however, are always the same. Nothing comes easily or without trial, often characterized by significant personal loss, sacrifice, or suffering. The leitmotif is that, in the end, such loss may be equally or more important to the searcher than the object associated with the end of the quest. Heroes are tested and often, like Odysseus's crew, found wanting. Often, the quest becomes the end in itself, as in the case of Moses, who wandered the desert for 40 years on a quest for a promised land he could not enter. Some quests are external, like the Celtic hero Peredur or his French and German equivalents Perceval and Parzival, all of whom sought the Holy Grail. Others are highly internalized, like Siddhartha's quest for enlightenment under the Bodhi tree.

Author and filmmaker Phil Cousineau describes Joseph Campbell's hero myth as a "monomyth." Commenting on Campbell's treatment of the hero, Cousineau writes:

> The monomyth is in effect a metamyth, a philosophical reading of the unity of humankind's spiritual history, the story behind the story. To paraphrase the ancient Japanese koan, it is the sound of one myth clapping: the universal quest for self-transformation. The journey of the hero is about the courage to seek the depths; the image of creative rebirth; the eternal cycle of change within us, the uncanny discovery that the seeker is the mystery which the seeker seeks to know. The hero journey is a symbol that binds, in the original sense of the word, two distant ideas, the spiritual quest of the ancients with the modern search for identity, "always the one, shape-shifting yet marvelously constant story that we find."[10]

The Hero's Quest is not that much different from how many of us approach our careers, how entrepreneurs approach competition, and even how brands compete in the market.

If all this seems like too much of a stretch to you, and you're not willing to wait until the next chapter, think of the way the myth of Thomas Edison has been used to retell the Hero's Quest in industrial terms. Search the Internet, and you'll find any number of "sources"—there goes that tricky Abolition of Context again—who will "verify" the number of times Thomas Edison failed to invent a light bulb. We stopped our sampling with 499 (a precise but inaccurate number) on the low side and 12,000 (an impressive, but equally incorrect number) on the high side. We could have kept going, but we didn't see the point. As Edison himself said, "Results? Why, man, I have gotten lots of results! If I find 10,000 ways something won't work, I haven't failed. I am not discouraged, because every wrong attempt discarded is often a step forward...."[11] And, after those 10,000 failures, Edison returns from the realms of imagination and experimentation with gifts in the form of 1,093 patents to, in Joseph Campbell's words, "...bestow boons on his fellow man"—the phonograph, the light bulb, the motion picture camera, and last, but hardly least, the electric chair.

Thomas Edison's story is a great example of how the Hero's Quest has been used as a cornerstone for a business history and tradition. It's also, to a fairly large degree, a nearly equally great example of successful corporate fiction. In point of fact, many of Edison's patents were for variations on other people's existing inventions or innovations, and much of the real work was done by his staff rather than the master himself. The story of Edison as lone genius wrestling the raw materials of nature into technological "booms" for humanity has proved more popular than the truth—hardly a first, or last, in the annals of business storytelling.

Creation Stories

Who am I? Where did I come from? Why am I here? To whom do I owe loyalty, and who owes loyalty to me? The answers to these questions are central to our understanding of ourselves and our immediate and extended worlds. It's no surprise, therefore, that myths and stories of creation are the most universal of them all. Throughout history, people have recognized that it is not only critical to understand that the past had a beginning but to be able to think about that beginning in a manner that lays a foundation for the future.

Every culture has sought to derive meaning and direction from its origin story, whether it is the Blackfeet story of the Old Man who wandered up to the prairies from the south, creating and arranging nature as he went along, or the Chinese legend of the creator goddess Nü Wa and her husband Fu Xi, or Maori tales of Rangi, the sky goddess, and Papa, the earth goddess. The notion of origins has dynamic and critical implications for any number of corporate activities from branding and creating corporate identity right down to developing both the ability and credibility to transfer intellectual property through licensing and franchise. The bottom line—and we mean that quite literally in this case—where you come from has everything to do with where you can go.

Again, we'll examine the business implications of these stories in greater depth in Chapter 7, but for now let's consider 10 highly marketable elements that can be tied directly to stories of creation.

Creation-Related Claim	Business Example
Authenticity	Coca-Cola: "It's the real thing."
Authority	"You're in good hands with Allstate."
Continuity of tradition	"Family owned and operated since...."
Credibility (validation over time)	"Established...."

73

Creation-Related Claim	Business Example
Acknowledged source of innovation	"At G.E., we bring good things to life."
Kinship	"Kraft Foods Inc.—The World's Favorite Foods."
Collective strength	"The Power of Blue."
Growth and evolution	"Dow—Living Improved Daily."
Originality	"Victorinox—The Original Swiss Army Knife."

Stories of Transformation

The notion of transformation is a subtext to many larger themes found in mythology, folklore, fairy tales, and literature. Transformation is often one of the end products of the Hero's Quest. It can also sometimes be a punishment, as in the case of werewolves and other wer-animal legends and the story of the fall of Adam and Eve, who were transformed into mortal flesh. At other times, transformation is a way of reconciling conflict. Sometimes, as in the case of the story of Eos, several elements of the transformation motif combine in a single story.

Eos, a goddess cursed by Aphrodite to only love mortal men, fell in love with Tithonus, a handsome prince from Troy. Tithonus begged Aphrodite for the gift of eternal life but forgot to ask for eternal youth and vitality. Tithonus continued to age and grew increasingly infirm while Eos remained eternally young. Tithonus begged for death, which was beyond even Zeus' power to grant. Eos solved the problem by transforming her lover into a grasshopper.

Transformation stories can be positive, as you will see in Chapter 7 in the stories of Nokia and General Electric, or less than positive, as in the case of the large body of global "Trickster" stories. The archetype of the Trickster (which we examine in greater

74

depth later in this book) is the embodiment of the notion of transformation, a character who shifts shapes and identities on a whim or to promote his or her own self-interests.

Cynics might argue that the Trickster has been reified in business disciplines such as advertising and marketing. Before we start getting hate mail from the American Marketing Association, consider this observation by Lewis Hyde, perhaps America's preeminent expert on Trickster mythology and stories:

> Gary Lindberg, in a fine book on confidence games as an American literary theme, has offered a useful definition of a confidence man: A confidence man is someone who is in the business of creating belief. That is to say, the confidence man is not necessarily a crook, which is why he is so problematic. Some creators of belief are the real thing—prophets, idealists, charismatics, inspiring politicians, and so forth. Land speculators in the nineteenth century were in the business of creating belief ("Come to New Jerusalem, Minnesota, where the town square will soon bustle, the fountains flow, the children laugh and the spacious parks!"). Some were the real thing (P. T. Barnum created East Bridgeport, Connecticut, this way), and others were con men in the criminal sense, creating only rude awakenings.[12]

Creating confidence isn't necessarily a bad thing, of course, or necessarily a precursor to unethical business practices.

Amadeo Peter Giannini, 1870–1949, who opened the Bank of Italy in a former San Francisco saloon on October 17, 1904, refused to let a little thing like the San Francisco earthquake of 1906 get in his way. To instill confidence in his bank in the quake's immediate wake, Giannini set up a "desk" made up of two barrels and a plank in the middle of the street and "opened" for business. In 1928, the Bank of Italy officially became the Bank of America. Giannini, who remained the bank's chairman until retiring in 1945, is credited with the invention of many modern banking practices, including the idea of a multiregional banking network and offering banking services tailored to meet the needs of middle-class Americans as well as those of the rich.

On the other hand, we have a parade of seeming confidence builders led by former Tyco chairman Dennis Kozlowski, former WorldCom, Inc. chairman Bernard Ebbers, former HealthSouth chairman Richard Scrushy, and former Enron chairman Kenneth Lay that serves as a silent warning about too much faith in certain business leaders.

Myths of the Fall and Redemption

You don't need to look much past the major religious doctrines of the West to discover stories of man's fall and redemption. The idea of collapse and renewal lies at the heart of Judeo-Christian tradition—the fall of Adam and the coming of a Messiah who will redeem Adamic sin are central to both Judaism and Christianity. But this theme isn't confined just to religion. Prometheus fell from grace with the gods and was ultimately redeemed by Hercules. Innocence is lost (the fall), wisdom is gained (redemption).

Redemption is the compensation for the fall, assuming you're lucky. If you're not lucky, you can always hope it at least earns you a lower sentence.

Martha Stewart is the poster child for how to transform a fall into career renewal. She's the latest in a long line of power-mad penitents stretching from the unrepentant former Nixon staffer Gordon Liddy and publicly repentant ex-Tyco boss Kozlowski to the piously repentant Rev. Ted Haggard.

Lots of companies have come back stronger from a fall, but perhaps none as strongly as Johnson & Johnson. J&J emerged as the paragon of corporate concern and a selfless guardian of the public health after seven people died on Chicago's west side in the fall of 1982 after taking Extra-Strength Tylenol tablets laced with 65 milligrams of cyanide, or 10,000 times the lethal dose. Before the tampering scare was over, 270 additional incident reports were filed, the majority of which were never substantiated. Quick action by the company in the form of a national recall of all products resulted in the brand remaining a viable player in the analgesic market to this day and Johnson & Johnson gaining a permanent place in business school crisis curriculums.

The Myth of the Crossroads

Crossroads myths center around the criticality of choice. The crossroads is a place where the unknown is met, fear is confronted and either wins or is vanquished, and where critical choices are made. Crossroads should never be thought of as the end of a journey, but they are critical interruptions.

Historically, physical crossroads have been regarded as sacred places. In Peru's Andes and in Siberia, for instance, travelers leave votive stones at a crossroads. Over time, these piles of stones have evolved into mini-pyramids.

In ancient Rome, the crossroads idea became the core of the festival of *Lares Compitales*, which was held every January. In India, Vedic marriage rituals offered special hymns that the bridal procession sang if the path from a bride's home to the new home where she was to live with her husband happened to go past a crossroads. In Greek mythology, Hecate was known as the goddess of the crossroads in line with her role as mistress of the three worlds—heaven, the earth, and the underworld. In more modern times, crossroads have been a place for occult ceremonies.

Whether you're running a business or just working inside one, you probably face a crossroads every day. And, as you'll see in Chapter 7, the lessons of all crossroads myths is that choices aren't always clear. In the next chapter, we apply the elements of these stories to real-world business models.

As you read through this analysis, don't lose sight of our main point: Storytelling needs to become a conscious element of your business planning and execution process. The stories we are looking at are only examples of how historical stories and myths can be used to develop effective business tools. These aren't the only stories, themes, or myths that you can use; they are just the ones we happened to select, because we believe they have a broad applicability to a variety of businesses.

The context in which business is conducted has changed dramatically since these stories were first told and, if we're right, may be on the verge of being functionally abolished, but the lessons these stories offer remain constant over time. Once again, it is incumbent on us as corporate storytellers and mythologists of commerce to find effective ways of telling them.

he tension in the room had already been as deep as the memory of a lost first love when Marshall entered the room. Now, 10 minutes later, the room's toxic ambience threatened to drag him down slowly, crushing him beneath itself like some kind of atmospheric quicksand. "I'm losing," he thought to himself. "I'm losing and I haven't even begun the pitch."

"Mr. Marshall, I'm sure you understand why you're here, although to be honest, I'm not entirely sure in my own mind why the rest of the committee thought you might even be a candidate to handle our, um, situation," said the balding man in the pinstriped, gray Baroni suit. "We've had everyone of any consequence sitting in that very chair you currently occupy," he continued. "The usual suspects, of course—Omnicom, WPP, and Interpublic—and even some of our global friends like Clemenger of Melbourne, LB Icon from Stockholm, Havas of Suresnes, Dentsu from Tokyo, and Cheil of Seoul. But none of them has brought us the kind of answer the committee is searching for. That's why certain individuals in this room thought it might be novel to try what I'm sure you would refer to as an 'out of the box' idea like interviewing some virtually unknown hotshot with a dubious client list. Someone, in short, exactly like you."

"Actually Mr. Bronstein, our client list..." Marshall began.

"Your client list, young man, if aggregated, would constitute less than a rounding error on the Abel Technologies' balance sheet," interrupted Bronstein, the longstanding CFO and—in the wake of the unexpected death of John Abel—acting CEO of Abel Technologies. "We have a serious marketing problem on our hands. I hardly think it's appropriate to call in, what did *Advertising Age* call you? Oh yes, 'the Viral King.' And, what was it *Brandweek* said? Let me see," Bronstein said shuffling through the papers in front of him. "Ah, here it is. 'Marshall's stealth marketing—his mastery of otherwise unacknowledged intuitive communication factors—allows his clients to spread their messages without the target audience knowing they're being contacted.' Very impressive if we were trying to launch a bioterrorist attack I'm sure, but we're a Fortune 10 company, not like your other clients. What you do may work for doubling the market share of some Costa Rican homebrew or getting attention for some offbeat designer who is happy if they sell 10 dresses a season or put some new hot spot or rock band on the map, but tell me, what do you think you can do for us?"

Marshall knew it was now or never. Bronstein was right. He and his small, tight-knit group of coconspirators at The Marshall Plan had never pitched a client a tenth the size of Abel Technologies before. But, here he was. Landing Abel could make his future. Losing it would just prove what Bronstein had suggested—that he wasn't ready for the big leagues and maybe never would be. Hell, he thought, I've got nothing to lose.

"Let me see if I can read between the lines of your RFP," he began, aware that his voice had seemed to develop a tremolo he had never heard before. "You say you're looking for a brand enhancement program. Actually, as we say in our proletarian circles, that's a load of crap. Everyone in the software industry knows two things about Abel Technologies. First, John Abel was responsible for 100 percent of the product development. And second, while it's true you have buildings full of potential Nobel laureates on the payroll, Abel hired them so nobody else could have them. Most of them are probably designing some quantum-level video game to amuse themselves. Nothing happened here without your founder's direct permission. He was a micro-managing megalomaniac. The only person he ever seemed to trust at all was that goon he kept around as a 'personal negotiator.' I notice you wasted no time dumping him; oh, excuse me, pensioning him off. You've only had one story—the John Abel story—such as it was, and now that's gone. Software distributors hate you, and your client list, while impressive if you don't mind the occasional drug lord or two, resents the stranglehold you have on them. You called me because, much as they lust after the billable hours, none of the big boys wants to take a risk on a company that's literally crumbling as we speak. Am I making myself clear, Mr. Bronstein?"

What might have passed as a thin smile on a face other than Bronstein's seemed to appear and then vanish. "Very impressive, Mr. Marshall," the executive said. "Very impressive indeed. Let's say, just for the sake of argument, you're partially right about us. Solving the problem of stopping the stock slide and repositioning us could be worth several small fortunes. Hell, boy, it's literally worth the net worth of this company. Not, of course, that we're offering it. So, I assume you came here prepared to do something a little more complicated than having some half-assed beautiful people show up in a new nightclub or request some liquor that's not on the market yet because the importer is undercapitalized."

"Not more complicated. Less," Marshall said. He could feel the bile climbing its way up his esophagus. This was it. It either worked and he was rich or it didn't and he went back to sweating the bills each month. "I'm proposing we tell the unknown story of John Abel. Fortunately, the real article is no longer with us, so we can say what we want without fear of contradictory behavior getting in the way. It's a simple story really, of a somewhat lonely boy who knew there was great power in having and keeping a secret and who dreamed of one day keeping all the most important secrets in the world.

"It's that vision that drove young Johnny to Grandma and Grandpa Abel's garage," Marshall continued. "That garage became first a refuge for a frightened boy with big dreams and then the base for a young entrepreneur. The boy grew, and slowly, the vision became a product. In time, as everyone knows, that product became the cornerstone of a global digital empire, an empire based on keeping secrets."

"Let's say that plays for a moment," Bronstein said, beginning to shut the file. "We're still too dammed dependent on little Johnny or John Abel the entrepreneur. So, your little story works against us. You've really given us a much nicer version of the same crap everyone else is trying to sell us. Our brand can't rest on the shoulders of a dead man, especially a dead man who was vilified behind his back."

"Couldn't agree with you more," Marshall said, a surprising confidence creeping into his voice. "Instead of dodging the fact that the death is a problem, we celebrate it."

"What kind of drugs are you on, son?" Bronstein said, as much to himself as anyone else.

"No drugs, just hear me out," Marshall countered. "We say that John Abel knew he wasn't immortal and actually cared what happened to the company after he died. It's a stretch, but it's all we've got. Then we say that for the past few years he began preparing for this day. At first his natural entrepreneurial bent made it hard for him to see the answer, but slowly it dawned on him. Abel Technologies wasn't just in the business of keeping secrets; it was in the business of defining what a secret is. Before John Abel, it was almost impossible to keep anything secret unless you were the only one who knew it. That's basically what your software does; it constantly generates random algorithms that can be accessed only by one person in an organization. Am I right?"

Bronstein just nodded. "Well, that's the beauty of this story," Marshall said. "That's the old model of a secret, and it worked well, but now Abel Technologies will broaden the traditional understanding of what a secret is. Your brilliant army of researchers will be the first organization in history in which many people can keep a secret. We can't perfect version 18.0 of John's software without John, but I bet all those future Nobel Prize winners might be able to come up with a fresh wrinkle or two. We'll stick to the original story, but we'll transfer the magic from John Abel the man to Abel Technologies the company. The company that continues to grow his legacy. No John? No problem."

No one said a word. Finally, Bronstein broke the silence. "So, we move from a paranoid person to perfected product. Is that your idea, Mr. Marshall?"

Marshall closed up his computer, his PowerPoint slides unseen. "Yes, that is my idea Mr. Bronstein."

Bronstein looked over the faces of the committee. "Well, there's no point discussing this any further," he said. "As the Old Man used to say, 'I may not want to invite you over for dinner, Mr. Marshall, but I'll be happy to put enough cash in your pocket so you can buy your own food for a long, long time. You've got a deal. It's a hell of a story."

Chapter 7

FIVE STAGES OF BUSINESS EVOLUTION

"Everything is held together with stories. That is all that is holding us together, stories and compassion."

—Barry Holstun Lopez, from an interview in *Poets and Writers*, Vol. 22, Issue 2 (March/April, 1994)

Everyone, and everything, has stories. You have stories. Your family has stories. Your neighborhood has stories. Your nation has stories. Your town or city has stories. The company you work for, or founded, or run has stories. The products, brands, and services you offer have stories. Viewed from a certain perspective, life and business are just exercises in collecting and editing stories, in building personal and commercial mythologies—nothing more and certainly nothing less. Too often, this collection and editing process is random or unconscious. That's where problems start and opportunities are lost.

So, how do you begin to make the process of self-mythologizing and storytelling conscious and purposive? One way might be to examine the library of literature that's been created in pursuit of the collection, codification, and analysis of mythology, fairy tales, folklore, legends, and other forms of storytelling. Of course, that will take at least a lifetime, and we doubt your business challenges will wait for you to complete your reading in the classics and anthropology. If you do take the time to read even some of the experts, you'll find surprisingly little agreement.

Formal scholars of the varieties of storytelling often classify the kinds of stories by their social functions. Some scholars argue that myths direct rites, rituals, and ritualistic behaviors, whereas legends are vehicles for transmitting historical knowledge. Others say that the label of tales or folktales is rightly confined only to stories about the relationship of man to animals and other aspects of the physical world. By similar logic, fables are moral or ethical stories aimed at directing behavior. Plain old "stories" serve a variety of functions, from entertainment to instruction. That kind of microsegmentation might be useful for academics, but for our purposes, we urge you to steal a good story wherever you find it, whether that be in a piece of classical world literature or in a comic book.

This isn't to say a formal study of storytelling can't be useful. Consider this observation from American folklorist John Greenway, who wrote, "As a culture achieves greater control over its environment, as the society moves from primitiveness to sophistication, the sacred recedes from the profane, into the past, into a world apart.... In those rare ecological situations where a people wins the struggle for subsistence but for some reason does not take the final step into civilization, myth, though no longer serving its primary function, may run wild, as if all the society's energy were channeled into its development."[1] And nowhere do myths run wilder or faster than in cyberspace.

Greatly aided and abetted by Adobe Photoshop, the Internet not only contributes to the acceleration of the Abolition of Context, but it also spawns its own myths and legends. There are literally thousands of examples we could cite here, but one of our favorites is the totally mythic "Tourist of Death."[2] The point, of course, is that the Internet makes it possible not just to create and globally distribute a story—but, as in the case of the "Tourist of Death," to also manufacture evidence in support of a story. This isn't necessarily good news for businesses. If commercial enterprises aren't very good at telling their own stories, their detractors clearly are.

"Big, global brands," Eamonn Kelly has observed, "are conspiracy's most common target."[3] Intrigued by Kelly's example of the disruption to Coca-Cola by rumors that it had hired right-wing death quads to quell labor unrest in Colombia, we searched Google for "Coca-Cola + Death Squad." At this writing, there were still 490,000 references to the story Coca-Cola officials have dismissed out of hand. Following another Kelly lead, we searched for links between Caribou Coffee and Islamic terrorists. Our search revealed a modest 24,000 references. The basis of the alleged linkage? Eighty-eight percent of Caribou is owned by the investment arm of the First Islamic Bank of Bahrain.

Nothing dies in cyberspace. We also searched Google for other anti-company myths and found a relatively modest 11,000 hits for "Procter & Gamble + Satanism" and an amazing 89,000 hits for "Procter & Gamble + the Devil." Procter & Gamble isn't the only company with an Internet reputation for being tight with Satan. According to other websites, the Illuminati, thanks to the Rockefeller family's interest in Exxon and the Chase Manhattan Bank, are ardent contributors to Dollars for Demons.[4] And let's not spare big drug companies such as Pfizer, which many Internet sites credit with leading the global mind-control agenda.[5] We could, unfortunately, go on almost forever. It's hard enough figuring out how to tell your own story without having to worry about refuting somebody else's story about you.

Businesses pass through life stages or evolutionary cycles just like individuals and societies. We could argue—stretching John Greenway's observation far past anything he had in mind—that Western commercial society had gained all but perfect control over its environment during the twentieth century but that as we've moved into the Information Age (or as some would have it the Post-Information Age), we haven't gained control of our collective mythologies. We've lost the thread of our own stories. Each of these business life stages can be paired to one of the five critical stories we discussed in the preceding chapter. Or, put another way, there are classic storytelling themes that can help a company understand both its internal and external position at every point in its life cycle.

As you'll see in succeeding chapters, when these stories address an internal audience, they can be adapted to explain and reinforce core values and ethical and market positions, and even clarify future corporate goals. They can be both didactic and inspirational. When targeted at an external audience, these stories can be used to build the basis of everything from brand identity to corporate mission. In this chapter, we examine each of our critical stories, often based on classic myths, and see how they match with key moments in a business history. The following chart recaps the five basic story lines outlined in Chapter 6, "Five Critical Story Themes," and matches them with what we see as the five parallel stages of business evolution.

Critical Story	Stage of Business Evolution
The Hero's Quest	The Entrepreneurial Vision
Creation Stories	The Establishment of the Enterprise
Stories of Transformation	The Corporate Coming of Age
Stories of the Fall and Redemption	The Crisis Phase
The Myth of the Crossroads	The Transition Phase

The Entrepreneurial Vision

Every business, large and small, began as a vision in the mind of its founder or founders. This vision—of a product, a service, or an unmet market demand—is the bedrock of all successful, and not so successful, business ventures. Whether a spark of imagination, a bit of fevered inspiration, or the calculated rational analysis of business conditions, it is the necessary precondition for all business formation. This vision can be the product of accident or design. It can emerge in response to a crisis or even as part of an academic exercise. Its goal can be to build a better world or just make a buck.

We see the story of this entrepreneurial vision pairing up almost perfectly with the Hero's Quest. Every entrepreneur we've ever met started off by looking for something and generally taking the long way around to find it. Consider the Reverend Samuel T. Cooper (retired), who back in 1876 discovered that lumberjacks often suffered from blisters and serious foot infections as a direct consequence of wearing poorly made wool socks. His pastoral concern, and his keenly honed sense of right and wrong, led the good reverend to start up his own hosiery business, S. T. Cooper and Sons, in a converted livery stable. Business boomed as word spread that the Cooper brand stood for unparalleled quality. By the early years of the twentieth century, the company had expanded into the underwear business. You may never have heard of Reverend Cooper or S. T. Cooper and Sons, but you undoubtedly know the contemporary fruit of Cooper's labor—the Jockey brand.

As Jockey's official history explains, "In 1909, one of our designers awoke in the middle of the night with a striking new underwear concept. Afraid that he might lose the inspiration, he woke his wife, and together they made a prototype. The finished product, eventually known as the KENOSHA KLOSED KROTCH, offered a convenient diagonal opening in place of the bulky, bunching drop-seat common to union suits. The new design revolutionized the union suit business."[6]

"We changed the world's underwear in 1934 when one of our designers created a strange, new kind of underwear called 'the brief,'" the history continues. "Unlike any underwear at that time, it provided men with 'masculine support,' available at that time only through the use of an athletic supporter, sometimes called a 'jock strap.' To discretely describe the function of the new-fangled underwear, we called it the Jockey (JOCK-ey) brief. Today, Jockey is a recognized trademark in over 120 countries."

And so you have it—the commercial incarnation of the Hero's Quest, which begins as a minister's vision of helping his fellow man, spiked by impassioned inspiration and sharpened by superior design. Health morphed to comfort morphed to fashion. It's a pretty credible story, don't you think?

Or consider the case (if you'll pardon the pun) of Jones Soda's founder Peter Von Stolk, who once said, "The Jones Soda story is really one of determination and fighting through challenges that most companies would never have to. No one's given us anything. Everything we've done; we've had to fight for, probably harder than we should have."[7] In his early twenties, Von Stolk realized he would never achieve his dream of becoming a professional skier. Having sworn up and down to his father that he didn't need a university education, Von Stolk was stuck looking for a way to prove his point. The initial answer came in the form of fresh-squeezed Florida orange juice. The young Canadian entrepreneur sold his car to raise the money for his first import order. In time, the orange juice business grew into an alternative beverage distribution business, Urban Juice and Soda Company, Ltd., and eventually into the Jones Soda company we know today.

Von Stolk sent the first case of Jones Soda to Nike's founder Phil Knight, an homage, we think, to the notion of the sports-oriented rebel who's not afraid of taking on the big boys. Von Stolk defines Jones Soda as a lifestyle company, and the lifestyle in question is definitely youth oriented, in your face, and unapologetic. Von Stolk has been quoted saying things like, "If you don't like Jones Soda, if you're not into it, I don't give a rat's ass. I'm not going to change my formula to please you.... If you are always trying to cater to all of the customers you have, you have no soul. You have to define yourself."[8] As Von Stolk tells it, that search for self is never over, a position he might share with Bill Strickland.

Strickland is the organizational and spiritual head of the Manchester Craftsmen's Guild and the Bidwell Training Center, Inc., in Pittsburgh's north side. These programs train inner-city residents to (among other things) read, grow orchids, work in the chemical industry, troubleshoot computers, and most recently, launch one of America's most successful music labels. Strickland has described his moment of enlightenment in terms that could have come straight out of classical mythology.

As he tells the story before audiences from the poorest of houses to the White House, his Hero's Quest started back in 1963.[9] At the time, Strickland was a 16-year-old near dropout in Pittsburgh's inner-city school system. One day as he was wandering the halls getting ready to skip school, he happened to look into an open classroom door and saw what for him became a defining transformational mystery, a potter turning a mound of clay on his potting wheel. "If ever in life there is a clairvoyant experience, I had one that day," he said in an interview. "I saw a radiant and hopeful image of how the world ought to be. It opened up a portal for me that suggested that there might be a whole range of possibilities and experiences that I had not explored. It was night and day—literally. I saw a line and I thought: This is dark, and this is light. And I need to go where the light is."[10]

Each of these vision tales tells us as much about the future as it does about the past. In Jockey's case, reliability, inspiration, and design expertise hold out the promise of a more comfortable, durable clothing line, based on the initial sense of caring, knowledge of, and respect for the customer embodied in the vision of a retired minister who couldn't stand the idea of working men suffering as a result of poor-quality goods. In the Von Stolk vision story, being actively engaged in pursuit of an independent lifestyle becomes the cornerstone of a maverick soft drink company or whatever Jones evolves into.[11] And finally, Bill Strickland's message of the power of personal transformation allows Manchester Bidwell (the parent organization of the two groups he heads) to reach 3,200 schoolchildren a year, train 500 full-time students every year, and launch into successful business venture after successful business venture. Strickland has already expanded his model of inner-city transformation to San Francisco, Cincinnati, and Grand Rapids.

The Establishment of the Enterprise

Stories about how businesses were built form capitalism's creation mythology. They set the backdrop for how companies want to be thought of by their employees and their customers. Consider Baileys Irish Cream. The official history has it that a committee of senior managers in Gilbeys of Ireland was struggling with the idea of creating a unique beverage that would reflect Ireland's heritage and "...unparalleled agricultural and distilling traditions."[12] According to the origin myth, it took three years to figure out the drink's chemistry because whiskey and cream don't mix naturally. Today, this "authentic" and "traditional" Irish product is sold in more than 130 countries. Baileys is now the number six global premium spirit brand and accounts for more than 55 percent of all spirits exported from Ireland, the nation that holds the number one position for largest per capita consumption—not bad when you consider 2,260 glasses of the stuff are consumed every minute of every day.[13] It's a touching history, but one contrarians challenge.

We remember a conversation, in Ireland, with Sir John Harvey-Jones, one of the most renowned figures in modern British business and a former member of the board of directors of Grand Metropolitan, one of Diageo's (the current owner of the Baileys' brand) forerunners. Sir John assured us that the real origins of the product lay in an attempt to resolve a simple business dilemma. At the time, Grand Met had a problem disposing of two surplus products—alcohol and Irish milk. According to Sir John, reducing the disposal costs—rather than the search for a drink that could embody traditional Irish roots—was the real motive force behind the creation of Baileys. Somehow it's an easier story to buy, although clearly not as an attractive story to sell.

The Corporate Coming of Age

We've paired the Corporate Coming of Age to the stories of transformation. How and why companies change can become the stuff of legend. Take Nokia, for example. Most people know Nokia as a manufacturer of cutting-edge telephones, but few realize that the original three companies that merged to form the current enterprise had their roots in forestry, rubber manufacturing, and cable manufacturing. According to Nokia, it was just a hop, skip, and a router from cutting down trees to making cell phones. As the company's British website boasts:

> From its inception, Nokia was in the communications business as a manufacturer of paper—the original communications medium. Then came technology with the founding of the Finnish Rubber Works at the turn of the 20th century.
>
> Rubber, and associated chemicals, were leading edge technologies at the time. Another major technological change was the expansion of electricity into homes and factories which led to the establishment of the Finnish Cable Works in 1912 and, quite naturally, to the manufacture of cables for the telegraph industry and to support that new-fangled device—the telephone![14]

So, you see the evolution from logging to logging on through your mobile was practically inevitable. That is, if you buy their version of the story. General Electric is another company that's found a way to reduce a complex corporate history into a simple story told through four short words: *Imagine, Build, Solve,* and *Lead.*[15] "In the end," the corporate website states, "our success is measured not only by our ability to think big, dazzling thoughts, but by our commitment to sweat the small stuff that brings ideas to life. It's a way—thinking and doing—that has been at the heart of GE for years."[16] Again, from filament to financial services suddenly seems like a simple turn of the page.

The Crisis Phase

The Crisis Phase of a business (and every business has at least one in its history) often echoes the stories of the fall/redemption. Businesses can, and do, enter into crisis at multiple points in their history. Often, this phase is reached when a business plateaus, as was the case in the early 1920s when Henry Ford, the man who as much as anyone invented the American automobile industry, began a long slide into jeopardy thanks to General Motors. Ford reached its plateau by the fiscal year ended February 29, 1924, when it was making $2 per unit on the Model T and car sales accounted for less than 5 percent of its profits.[17] Today's generation of the Ford family has its own opportunity to negotiate the choppy waters of the Crisis Phase.

The Transition Phase

The Transition Phase is entered every time a business, its board, or its CEO takes a firm stand in the face of an uncertain future. One could say that most businesses pass in and out of minor transition phases several times each week, if not several times each day. But the Transition Phase stories of legend are the big stories—the kind where a firm or its leader adopted a "bet the company" strategy when faced with a tough decision.

Let's contrast how two companies came to a similar place in their corporate lives and made very different choices.

We'll begin with Chrysler Corporation. The company had enjoyed record sales in 1972 and 1973. By the mid-1970s, however, the glory years looked like they were gone forever, and Chrysler was facing what it termed a "financial crisis." Enter Lee A. Iacocca, hired on November 2, 1978 as Chrysler's president and named the company's chairman just 10 months later, following the resignation of John J. Ricardo, the man who had recruited him to the company.

Iacocca slashed costs, restructured management, and brought new faces into the executive offices, but nothing seemed to work.

Faced with ongoing financial pressure, unrelenting assaults from offshore competition, declining consumer demand for Chrysler products, and a growing consumer impression that Chrysler wasn't producing quality cars any longer, Chrysler needed money to stay afloat and to finance the programs Iacocca believed could turn the company's fortunes around. Iacocca found himself facing a series of personal and professional crossroads.

He had enjoyed a prosperous 32-year run at the Ford Motor Company. Conceivably, he could have walked away from Chrysler, blaming the situation on his predecessors, the high cost of gasoline, and excessive government regulation. He could have announced that he needed more time with his family, or to pursue "other interests." He could have stayed in a state of denial until the company collapsed or the board threw him out with a golden parachute tucked under his arm.

Instead, he did something few executives have ever done: He decided to come clean with the public and ask the government for help. Iacocca asked federal lawmakers to guarantee Chrysler's loans. No money ever changed hands between the government and the company, but on January 7, 1980 President Jimmy Carter signed into law the Chrysler Corporation Loan Guarantee Act, which had been passed by Congress the month before. The new law gave the company $1.5 billion in federal loan guarantees.

Iacocca then took his case to the American people. Admitting the company hadn't always lived up to its claims, the Chrysler chairman took to the airwaves in July 1980. Staring into the camera, the picture of avuncular trust and sincerity, Iacocca uttered what became his trademark challenge, "If you can find a better car...buy it." The company survived, and Iacocca moved into that tight circle of CEOs, such as Bill Gates, Warren Buffet, and Jack Welch, who are both business giants and genuine media celebrities.

Not all visits to the corporate crossroads are quite as successful.

Hudson Foods was seen as dragging its feet during a 1997 recall of actual and potentially contaminated ground beef, a recall that turned into the largest meat recall in American history. In 1999, a federal grand jury found the company not guilty of lying to government inspectors during the recall, but the commercial damage was already done. Hudson Foods lost the Burger King account, its single largest customer, and eventually sold out to Tyson.

History repeated itself in 2006, this time in the produce department, when some spinach producers took a wait-and-see approach to recalling their product in the face of another contamination scare. Many restaurants removed spinach from their menus as the recall played itself out, and some never put it back.

We've now seen how certain classic story lines can be applied to specific businesses. In the next chapter, we look at examples of how some fed or destroyed companies.

The old man shuffled into the penthouse boardroom with an equal mix of confidence and weariness. He stared at the thick teak conference table. The grain of the wood had been accentuated by thousands of polishings, its suppleness preserved by generations of oilings, hand-rubbed to penetrate deep below the surface and renew the spirit of the wood.

He scanned the faces before him—old men, some older than him but, unlike him, afraid to show their years, seeing age as a sign of weakness. Around the table were a sprinkling of younger faces, masked souls as old as the others, souls that had aged because they knew no joy.

The uniform lines of the room's oak-paneled walls were randomly interrupted by works of art. The old man knew nothing about this kind of art, but he knew it was here because it was expensive, not because anyone liked it or because it held any special meaning for them.

He shifted uncomfortably, his muscular bulk barely contained by the new suit his wife had insisted he buy for this occasion and this occasion alone. He would never wear it again, seeing it now as a uniform of an army he would never join. Pressed to service in such an army, the old man knew he would desert. To stay in a place like this, with comrades such as this, would be to die not at the hands of an enemy but slowly by attrition at the hands of people you believed to be your friends.

"We're so glad you could be with us today," said one of the soulless men sitting at the head of the table. "Please, join us."

"I'm not sure why I'm here," the old man said, his voice slightly cracked from a lifetime of speaking with the wind. Among his people, he was known as the wisest of the storytellers. These men, though, thought of him as a shaman, a man who spoke to spirits and knew the secrets of the world. His mind wandered back to the excited visit from his daughter, his favorite child who had broken his heart when she left to find a place in this world of concrete, steel, and glass. She worked for these men, and it was through her that he had been summoned to this room. There was no other reason for him to have come. "I am a simple man, and I live a simple life," he said. "How is it I can possibly be of service to you?"

"Oh, don't be so modest," said another of the soulless men, this one much younger than the first—at least on the outside—leading him to a chair at the front of the room. "Your daughter—quite an asset to the corporation by the way—has told us all about your work, and we believe you're just the fellow we're looking for." His work? He didn't work in the sense these men worked. He lived, moving through life, doing what was required. His life was a link on a never-ending chain of privileged duty, nothing more and nothing less. He was a storyteller, like his father before him and his father's father's father before that.

"You see, we have a little business problem," another of the soulless ones went on.

"I know nothing of business," the old man said.

"But you do...ah...see things, don't you?" the man persisted.

"I see only what is given to me to see," the old man explained as he would to a child. "And what I see has nothing to do with business."

"Tell us what you see," said a softer voice. Squinting, the old man now saw there was a woman in the room. She was dressed like the men, but her spirit was stronger, clearer, more alive. "We want to know what you see in your dreams."

"I see our Mother Earth crying," the old man said, his voice full of sadness. "I see cuts on her body and poison in her blood. I see her children dying of hideous diseases—fat yet starving for the good things the Mother can provide. I see her choking on the air, sickened by the water, collapsing under the weight of the buildings of the cities. I see our Mother's life being drained out of her."

"Is there no hope?" the woman asked.

"Oh, there is always hope," the old man said. "What has been made wrong can be put right. Healing is as natural as death. But we must stop. No, you must stop. The drugs you make keep people from feeling what they are supposed to feel. They treat the surface but let the disease live deep inside the body. It attacks at will and then retreats back into its place of concealment. Your medicines do not heal; they just delay the inevitable."

"We cannot thank you enough for your time," the woman said. "Be assured your daughter will be rewarded for bringing you to our attention." Rewarded, the old man thought, what did these soulless ones know about rewards? He had come because his daughter, who valued their ways more than his, had asked. He had been honest, and now he was happy to be going home.

"Well, that was a waste of time," said one of the men after the old man had left the room. "I thought the old geezer was supposed to tell us about some healing wildflower we've never heard of. We can't make drugs out of dreams."

"Can't we?" the woman shot back. "Don't be a fool. The future isn't in the next product; it's in the next vision. I propose that we begin to look at a whole new line—medicines that enhance your awareness of your body, not just mask symptoms. The old man is right. Cities in the emerging world are full of children who are simultaneously suffering from malnutrition and obesity. And, look at our kids. Type II diabetes may be the AIDS of their generation, yet to us they appear healthy. The old man has given us the key. We can sell connectivity to the self and the earth. We'll own the market. We can use his story and that whole Mother Earth imagery to open up what amounts to a brand new industry."

Home again, the old man spoke to the spirits of his trip to the city. He told them about the soulless men and the woman who seemed different. "You have so much to learn still," the spirits whispered to him. "She, too, is soulless; she just has learned to hide it better. That's why they let her into their council in the first place." The old man thought about this and prayed to the spirits that his daughter would come home before she too lost her soul. He thought again about what he had seen, and he prayed harder than he had ever prayed before.

Chapter 8

Applied Storytelling 101: Industries

"To share our stories is not only a worthwhile endeavor for the storyteller,
but for those who hear our stories and feel less alone because of it."

—Joyce Maynard

"I am a teller of stories, a weaver of dreams. I can dance, sing, and in
the right weather I can stand on my head. I know seven words of Latin,
I have a little magic, and a trick or two. I know the proper way to meet a
Dragon, I can fight dirty but not fair, I once swallowed thirty oysters in a
minute. I am not domestic, I am a luxury, and in that sense, necessary."

—John Hurt, The Storyteller, 1988

"Tell me, muse, of the storyteller who has been thrust to the edge of
the world, both an infant and an ancient, and through him reveal
everyman. With time, those who listened to me became my readers.
They no longer sit in a circle, but rather sit apart. And one doesn't know
anything about the other. I'm an old man with a broken voice, but
the tale still rises from the depths, and the mouth, slightly opened,
repeats it as clearly, as powerfully. A liturgy for which no one needs
to be initiated to the meaning of words and sentences."

—Homer, the aged poet in Der Himmel über Berlin, 1987

Good stories touch your imagination. Great stories steal your soul.

Good stories resonate with us and may even cause a tear to involuntarily form in the corner of our eyes. Great stories cause that twist of gut or bowel. They make our blood boil and drive us blindly into battle. Great stories fire our rage or bring us peace. They can inspire people, companies, movements, and sometimes even nations.

Good stories inspire action. Great stories build industries. A case in point is the aerospace industry, whose origins can be traced to the first time a human looked toward a bird and considered its biological advantages or turned his or her vision to the stars, the moon, the sun, and the planets and wondered if it were possible to reach something that appeared almost close enough to touch.

People have been telling stories about flying ever since people have told stories. And for just as long, they've been obsessed with the moon. Almost every culture has an active moon mythology. In Hinduism, *pitri-yāna*, "the way of the ancestors," leads to the sphere of the moon. Shiva, in his role as Transformer, carries a crescent moon as his emblem. One of the three traditional mid-autumn Chinese festivals is the festival of the moon goddess Heng-ugo. Altaic peoples prayed to new moons for blessings and luck. The Maya moon goddess Ixchel was both the constant companion and evil aspect of the sun god Kinich Abau.

But it wasn't until the 1960s when man's obsession with flight, the moon, and a healthy dose of Cold War paranoid politics converged to build an industry out of several millennia of storytelling.

When John F. Kennedy made his famous speech of September 12, 1962, at Houston's Rice University, establishing manned flight to the moon as a top priority for the United States, he built his argument not with the rhetoric of Cold War competition or the threat of Soviet supremacy in space, but rather by telling the story of human history reduced to a few lines:

No man can fully grasp how far and how fast we have come, but condense, if you will, the 50,000 years of man's recorded history in a time span of but a half-century. Stated in these terms, we know very little about the first 40 years, except at the end of them advanced man had learned to use the skins of animals to cover them. Then about 10 years ago, under this standard, man emerged from his caves to construct other kinds of shelter. Only five years ago man learned to write and use a cart with wheels. Christianity began less than two years ago. The printing press came this year, and then less than two months ago, during this whole 50-year span of human history, the steam engine provided a new source of power.

Newton explored the meaning of gravity. Last month electric lights and telephones and automobiles and airplanes became available. Only last week did we develop penicillin and television and nuclear power, and now if America's new spacecraft succeeds in reaching Venus, we will have literally reached the stars before midnight tonight.[1]

That's not bad when you think about it—50,000 years of human history plus a political agenda all boiled down to a 185-word story. It was the compelling vision of this story that Kennedy used to frame his manned space flight agenda. Within the context of his story, the space race was as inherently American as baseball, assuming, of course, that you liked to think of America as a world leader, and who didn't in 1962?

"If this capsule history of our progress teaches us anything," Kennedy told that audience at Rice, "it is that man, in his quest for knowledge and progress, is determined and cannot be deterred. The exploration of space will go ahead, whether we join in it or not, and it is one of the greatest adventures of all time, and no nation which expects to be the leader of other nations can expect to stay behind in the race for space."[2] The President had tapped into two stories in his speech. The first was one of the oldest of all—the story of a man who could fly; the second was the myth of America's Manifest Destiny—this time extended from the coasts of the Atlantic and Pacific to the closest outposts of the frontiers of space and beyond. Obviously, Kennedy recognized a good story when he heard it.

But this is more than a quick case study in effective storytelling—it's a great example of how old stories and myths can be effectively recycled to address contemporary applications. Of course, not all the examples we can think of are as positive as the application of Manifest Destiny to the space race.

The Aerospace Industry: A Case Study

As we've said, stories can be used to create industries. And, as you'll see, they can also destroy them. It all depends on who's telling the story and who believes it.

Kennedy successfully used the metaphor of Manifest Destiny to mask what, in retrospect, cynics might see as a race for Cold War space supremacy. His speech was all the more effective because there was already a long tradition of human flight and moon exploration storytelling in place. By the 1960s, Americans—at least Americans of certain inclinations—were awash in a flood of science fiction stories and movies.

Many of the stories and concepts we've come to associate with science fiction are as old as literature itself. The mechanical servants found in Homer's *Iliad* bear an uncanny resemblance to our idea of robots. *Icaromenippos* or *Journey Through the Air,* ascribed to Lucian of Samosata (born circa C.E. 125), describes a journey to the moon made possible through the use of strapped-on wings. Wings weren't the only strap-ons on Lucian's mind. *Icaromenippos* also describes the existence of cyborgs, prosthetic limbs, and the moon dweller's custom of donning artificial private parts. Lunar visits (this time aided by bottles of dew and solar evaporation) were a key motif in Cyrano de Bergerac's 1657 *Voyage Dans La Lune* or *Voyage to the Moon.*

In the nineteenth and early twentieth centuries, popular authors, including Jules Verne and H. G. Wells, added to the growing canon of space literature. Both Verne's *De la Terre á la Lune* or *From the Earth to the Moon* (1865) and *Autour de la Lune* or *The Moon Voyage* (1869) and Wells's *The War of the Worlds* (1898) and *The First Men on the Moon* (1901) popularized the idea of space exploration. Even Edgar Rice Burroughs, best known as the creator of Tarzan, was an active promoter of the idea of space exploration. Starting in 1917, Burroughs published 11 titles in his John Carter of Mars series; five titles in his Venus series; and several nonseries looks on space travel, including *The Moon Maid* (1926), *The Moon Men* (1926), and *Beyond the Farthest Star* (1941).

In 1911, Hugo Gernsback, the publisher of *Modern Electronics* magazine, serialized what many consider to be the first true modern science fiction novel, *Ralph 124C41=: A Romance of the Year 2660*. In April 1926, Gernsback launched *Amazing Stories* magazine, the first magazine devoted to publishing "science fiction"— a term Gernsback coined after his original neologism, "scientification," proved less than popular.

The story of manned space flight was told over and over again. In January 1930, the first issue of the pulp magazine *Astounding* was published. In 1938, John W. Campbell became its editor, insisting that "hard science" be the basis for all submitted stories and ushering in what genre devotees refer to as "The Golden Age of Science Fiction." In what becomes science fiction's contribution to the life-mimics-art category, one of *Astounding*'s most devoted fans was Werner von Braun, mastermind of the German rocket program in World War II, who somehow managed to receive the magazine all through the war years.

It is perhaps no small irony that one of the most influential early advocates of manned space flight and lunar exploration in America was the German-born scientist/author Willy Ley, who, in addition to his more traditional scientific training and publishing, popularized the work of von Braun, worked with Walt Disney, and in his spare time, wrote science fiction stories. It was Ley's collected works—especially the books on space exploration aimed at grade schoolers and published in the 1950s— that helped convince a whole generation of Baby Boomers that space was the place and that their future was in the stars. Ley's work—both popular and scientific—painted a picture of a future where space stations orbited the earth and where the moon and even Mars could be explored and colonized.

Ley wasn't the only one to use fiction (in this case, science fiction) in the service of the furtherance of fact. The pantheon of modern storytellers who inflamed the imaginations of young Americans and focused their attention on the stars include such (now) establishment authors as Isaac Asimov, Robert Heinlein, and Ray Bradbury.

Sometimes the attraction of the world created in pulp science fiction classics such as *Amazing Stories* magazine drew people too far away from the science and too deeply into the fiction, as in the odd case of John Whiteside Parsons, one of the founders of Caltech's Jet Propulsion Laboratory.[3] But tragic figures like Parsons aside, there's little doubt about the power of those stories to create commercial empires.

Today, the plot line of those early science fiction stories is an industry active in more than 40 countries. In the United States alone, about 700,000 people are directly employed in aerospace. The European aerospace industry supports about 420,000 workers, and Canada, the sixth-largest aerospace producer in the world, employs an additional 85,000 workers. And the children of Verne and Wells have created not only industries, but legions of new product lines.

Spinoff, founded in 1976, is an annual NASA publication devoted to documenting the successful commercialization of NASA technology and typically features between 40 and 50 NASA-inspired products.[4]

Here are some of these products:

- **Space Shuttle spin-offs**—A miniaturized ventricular assist pump (artificial heart), NASCAR insulation, 30-second blood diagnostic tool, infrared camera, infrared thermometer, high-temperature jewelry design blocks, land mine removal devices, prosthesis materials, vehicle tracking systems, and video stabilization software

- **International Space Station (ISS) spin-offs**—SpiraFlex resistance exercise device, Zipnut, fast-cooking ovens, 360-degree camera, golf clubs with Zeemet inserts, and low-vision enhancement systems

- **Apollo spin-offs**—Computer-aided tomography technology, magnetic resonance imaging, cordless power tools, athletic shoe design, freeze-dried foods, and water purification technologies

We don't think that the authors of those early stories of space travel intended to create markets for long-driving golf clubs or freeze-dried foods, but the men and women who listened to those stories and heard them with their hearts as well as their minds have been responsible for creating the documented NASA technologies that have, in their wake, led to about 1,400 commercial products.

The story of flying to the moon is a great story. Had it only been a good story, perhaps we would have invested more heavily in terrestrial battlements and super weapons.

What John Kennedy knew that day in Houston was that it was a big enough story to capture and focus the energies of a nation, and in particular the younger generation. Being the first to the moon was more than a propaganda game, however. A country that could master the challenges posed by some of the oldest stories on Earth was, unquestionably, the most powerful nation.

When Apollo Commander Neil Armstrong set foot on the moon on July 20, 1969, he did more than take a small step for man and a giant step for mankind. He also wrote the final chapter in several of man's oldest tales.

Beyond the Final Frontier

Sometimes, of course, industries begin to believe their own mythologies or stories—generally with disastrous results. We don't feel the need to go into great length here, but we will cite a couple of examples that make our point.

The railroad industry, arguably once one of the most powerful, if not *the* most powerful, industries in America, saw itself as the master of continental travel. After all, it was the May 10, 1869 driving of the Golden Spike at or near Promontory Summit in Box Elder County in Utah by Leland Stanford, the president of the Central Pacific Railroad, that formally united the Atlantic and Pacific coasts, making transcontinental travel accessible. The railroad industry, so proud of its own story, refused to take the upstart automotive industry seriously as a competitor for both freight and passengers.

By the same token, traditional supermarket operators refused—and paradoxically still refuse—to see Wal-Mart as a viable direct competitor. In the early years, supermarket operators used to scoff at the idea that Wal-Mart could sell food at all, because it had no established history in food. Then, as Wal-Mart continued to put operators out of business and challenge the margin structure of the survivors, the industry conceded that the discounter might be a threat, but only because it enjoyed what were perceived as favorable labor rates. As late as 2003, Mark Tatge wrote on Forbes.com, "The widely held belief that Wal-Mart's grocery business is a deadly threat to established supermarket chains may only be a myth."[5] Interestingly, Tatge's observations came at a time when Wal-Mart was America's largest food retailer.

Clearly, sometimes believing your own story is the worst mistake you can make.

We want to make it clear that we are not saying the modern aerospace industry is a direct result of Mayan moon goddess myths or pulp stories in science fiction magazines. Nor are we saying that President Kennedy's desire to reach the moon first can be directly attributed to Jules Verne or Robert Heinlein. Obviously, the creation of an industry, or even a successful major repositioning of an industry, is the result of the interaction of any number of economic, technological, social, and often political forces.

Guidelines for Storytellers

What we are saying is that establishing a new industry is made easier by the conscious manipulation of aspects of storytelling. Here are a few broad guidelines that might help you in case you have a new industry in mind:

- **Guideline 1**—The establishment of a new industry involves the manipulation of several stories. Building a case for manned space flight to the moon played off an audience precondition toward and familiarity with stories about flight, the mystery of the moon, space travel, Manifest Destiny, and American pioneer and explorer legends.

- **Guideline 2**—It's critical that these strands of past stories be woven together to form what seems like an entirely new story. Many religions have been founded on past beliefs or by employing other religion's sacred sites, but it's important that these references to the past be used, *not* acknowledged. What made John Kennedy's call for manned flight to the moon convincing was not its relationship to a drive-in science fiction film, but his ability to cast his vision as unique and contemporary.

- **Guideline 3**—Big stories require big storytellers. When Moses came down from the mountain with the Ten Commandments, he didn't say he had thought them up, but rather that God had given them to him. By the same token, having the president of the United States say that we should send a man to the moon was far more convincing than having that same message delivered by scientists who spoke with odd accents or by eccentric science fiction writers.

- **Guideline 4**—Remember, inventing an industry is really hard work. There aren't that many people who have ever done it, and it is becoming more and more difficult to do every day.

- **Guideline 5**—Most of the time, creating an industry involves several individuals. The story of Genentech, for example, isn't the story of the biotechnology industry. That story can only be told when the Genentech story is combined with those of Immunex, Amgen, Biogen, and Monsanto, among others. By the same token, the Microsoft story isn't the story of the personal computing industry until it's combined with the stories of Apple, Xerox PARC, Intel, Sun Microsystems, Oracle, and literally dozens of other companies.

- **Guideline 6**—Stories supporting the creation of an industry have to be as inclusive as possible. There's a reason why Monsanto tied its genetically modified seed to the idea of eradicating world hunger and why Genentech spoke of a future where certain congenital disorders could be either rendered obsolete or addressed early on, rather than the profit potential of such ideas. By the same token, the early Internet and PC pioneers spoke about making information free and democratizing access to ideas rather than the potential for labor reduction and increasing workloads. And once again, manned flight to the moon was positioned as an extension of human potential, not an exercise in Cold War technological arm wrestling.

So, it isn't all that easy to tell the story of a brand new industry, unless that industry is really more of a modification of an existing industry, as in the case of cellular telephony or digital photography. In those cases, a much "smaller" story is needed—like the stories of corporations that we examine in the next chapter.

"*I* don't understand," a clearly frazzled Sam Brown said more to himself than to his companion as he poured over the results of his latest customer polling.

"Now, Sam, don't get yourself all worked up," warned Susan Ashby, his executive vice president of marketing.

"Is that your expert advice, Susan?" Brown shouted. "Read these verbatims. 'Allied remains one of the most trusted old names in our industry. Companies like Allied are the foundation on which this industry was built. Allied best embodies what I think about when I think about traditional thinking.' Hell, Susan, this is your job! Our customers think of us as a dinosaur. Strong? Sure, until a nimbler life form comes along. Big? Yeah, like that's a virtue in an industry where all the innovation is coming out of small, entrepreneurial shops. Traditional? Great, in an industry that's changing so fast it can't even catch its collective breath."

"Now, Sam, relax," Ashby said, turning to Brown. He had been Allied's CEO for three years, and if something didn't change fast, he wasn't going to be around to celebrate his fourth anniversary. "Oh, well," she thought. "He's a nice-enough guy, but CEOs come and go these days. It's just the way of the world." To Brown, she said, "I'm sure we can develop an actionable approach that we can proactively operationalize in our next media campaign. I'll just socialize these results with my staff and get back to you ASAP."

"Can't you even speak English?" Brown screamed. "For your information, actionable means capable of being litigated, not something one can take action on. You'd like to see us get sued, Susan? Is that it? Forgive me for not buying into the argument that shallow is the new deep. I need a new campaign and maybe a new EVP of marketing while I'm at it. Socialize that with your staff and, oh, Susan, be sure to get back to me whenever it's convenient."

Wraithlike, Ashby seemed to evaporate out of the room in one fluid motion, leaving Brown alone with his thoughts and doubts. Slowly he shut down his computer, as if to bury the bad news in digital limbo. What he desperately needed now was a moment of clarity, the kind gained for a brief, teasing moment with the first sip of a neat double 30-year-old Laphroaig and lost by the first deep swallow.

One thing was certain: If he spent one more minute trapped in his office, checking his BlackBerry with a frequency bordering on obsessive compulsion, he was going to go mad. He was 58, the wrong age to lose a CEO job. But facts were facts. He had barely stabilized Allied's share price at an anemic $16. The company—and maybe Brown himself—bored the analysts to death. The board was gradually turning on him. He had months left, maybe weeks. What he needed was a miracle. What he opted for was a walk to the park a block away from his office. Sitting on the first bench he came to, his eyes closed; the sun washing over his face, Brown was lost in thought. Opening his eyes, he discovered he had been joined by one of the legions of pigeon ladies who seemed to be hired by the city to populate the parks. "Having a tough day, are we?" the pigeon lady asked. "You know, my mother used to say, 'A problem shared is a problem cut in half.'"

"I wish that were true," Brown said. "But it's my job to solve problems, and this time I seem to have run into one I can't beat."

The pigeon lady stared at Brown. Nice man, she concluded, just making things too hard, like everybody else today. "Oh, can't be that bad," she said. "My mother always said it's a lot easier to solve somebody else's problems than it is to deal with your own. So, tell me, Mr. Businessman, what's on your mind?"

Hesitating, Brown finally said, "It's really complicated. You see, I run this large company. Eighty years ago, we practically invented our industry, but today everybody—especially the people we're trying to sell to—thinks of us as old fashioned and out of step. They have respect for what we were but contempt for what we are. If I don't figure out how to turn things around, I'll be joining you every day at this park."

"Are they right, these customers of yours?" the pigeon lady asked.

"No, they're not right," he snapped. "Look, let me tell you about Allied. We were one of the first companies in our business to understand the power of linking information and supply chains. We didn't just help people get things from place to place, we made them smarter in the process. Sure, we don't have fancy names for all of our service lines, but we have 80 years of solid, constant innovation behind us. Our problem is that we don't try to fool our customers into believing we can do things for them that we can't do. Our integrity is everything to us."

"That's a great story, mister," Brown's bench mate told him. "How come your customers don't believe it?"

Ironically, that was the question. "I don't know," Brown said. "I guess we just don't take the time to talk to our customers much. We're either selling them something, or bombarding them with collateral material they never even look at, or we're stuck in business reviews, but we don't seem to just talk much anymore."

"Well, Mother always said life is like marriage," the pigeon lady said, "if you don't remember to talk pretty soon you can forget about the other things. If I were you, I'd just call them up and tell them you want to hear what they're thinking about and see if you can help. Old-fashioned values don't have to be old fashioned. Not if you're living them instead of just reciting them."

"You know, you're right," Brown said, the memory of a neat double 30-year-old Laphroaig dancing fleetingly across his mind. "We've got a great story; we just have to get back to telling it. Say, excuse me, I'm terribly sorry, I haven't even introduced myself. I'm Sam Brown, and I run Allied right down the street."

"Pleased to meet you, Mr. Brown," the pigeon lady said, "I'm Elisa Michaels, same as I was born."

"Say. Ms. Michaels, I don't suppose you'd consider working with me, would you?" Brown asked. "I've been thinking of making some changes in my marketing department."

"Well, I don't know," Elisa Michaels said. "I'm retired for many years now, and I wouldn't want to be the cause of anyone else's misfortune...but I do get a bit bored. Could I still come and feed my friends?"

"Elisa, after what you've just given me, you can come to the park anytime you want. Just make sure to stop by my office and grab me on your way out. And don't ever take no for an answer," Brown said, escorting his new EVP of marketing back to work.

Chapter 9

APPLIED STORYTELLING 101: THE CORPORATION

"Vivid stories translate dry, abstract numbers into compelling pictures of how deep yearnings of decision influencers can come true."
—Jack Keen

"Audiences often don't want to be in control of a story. They want to be lost in your story. They come to hear you be the storyteller."
—Steven Spielberg

"The concept of a story may be a new idea to the boardroom, but storytelling is at least as old as the person who defined it as an art 2,400 years ago—Aristotle...But even Aristotle knew that not all stories are created equal."
—Cliff Atkinson

B efore we examine the mythology of corporations, it's fair to note that the idea of "the corporation" is in itself a kind of myth, a commercial folktale, an economic engine disguised as a fable. A corporation—or even its more accessible poor relation, a small company—is often spoken of as if it possesses a sentient existence of its own.

Ask yourself whether you've ever heard, or said, something like this: It's the company's position.... The company feels.... The company believes that.... Or, the company doesn't care about.... So and so was the face/voice of the company.... Odds are, you have, because we tend to ascribe anthropomorphic qualities to companies and corporations, and the larger they are, the more we treat them as independent beings.

Part of this might be human nature—our desire to reduce a large, faceless, powerful force down to a simple, single unit that can be affirmed or battled, loved or hated. Perhaps not so surprisingly then, most of the conversations you have about companies begin to sound like an oddly familiar story—the story of David and Goliath. This often poses a challenge, particularly when you're trying to sell the notion of a kind, sensitive company. Want a quick example to seal our point? Just consider how much resistance Wal-Mart encounters, especially in communities where it has no pre-existing corporate presence.

If the tendency to see legal constructs as larger-than-life antagonists is the bad news, the good news is that every entity—legal or biological—has a story and, with careful management, there's a chance you can get that story to work for you. How you tell that story, of course, has a major impact on how your story—and therefore your company—is received. Consider this contrast in the stories of two high-technology players, Apple and Microsoft.

The Microsoft Story

Log on to Microsoft's website and navigate to its corporate history section, and you'll find this positive kind of all-embracing, boy-next-door, we-can-do-it rhetoric:[1]

> To some, our company's early vision, "A PC on every desk and in every home," must have seemed like science fiction. But Bill Gates and Paul Allen, who cofounded Microsoft in 1975, were passionate about the same idea. They envisioned bringing computers to life by developing software, the instructions that make electronic devices work, that would make computing power accessible to everyone.

...in 1975, Bill Gates and Microsoft cofounder Paul Allen saw the potential to turn a hobbyist into something more.

At Microsoft, we believe that the true measure of our success is not just in the power of our software, but in the potential it unleashes in us all.... With great ideas—and great software—our future has no limits.

Now read this exciting version of the history of Apple, albeit, not Apple's official history:[2]

Following the historic visit to Xerox PARC in 1979, (Apple cofounder Steve) Jobs and several other engineers began to develop the Lisa, which would redefine personal computing. Jobs, however, proved to be a poor project manager, and was taken off the Lisa by Mike Markkula, then president of Apple, and one of the major stockholders.

Although a successful businessman, it soon became clear that [former Apple chairman and CEO John] Sculley did not know much about the computer industry.

Sculley began to lose interest in the day to day operations of Apple. Eventually the Apple Board of Directors decided they'd had enough.

...[Former Apple CEO Michael] Spindler, by all accounts, was the wrong man for the job. A fairly impersonal man, Spindler's office was nearly impossible to get into.

...[Former Apple CEO Gil] Amelio made a strong effort to bring Apple back to profitability, but his efforts would prove to be largely unsuccessful.

We have to hand it to whoever wrote the Apple history. They get an "A" for honesty, but based on how these stories are told, which company would you assume would be the most successful? We hope those guys at www.apple-history.com aren't planning on launching a brand promotion company next.

Interestingly enough, both companies' stories begin in much the same way—two friends, looking on as computer hobbyists were building what appeared to be a niche market at best, and seeing the foundation for not just a company, but a revolution in how people live their lives. That's where the similarity ends. The Microsoft story is one of devotion to the greater corporate good. The official Apple story is a chronicle of intrigue and internal power plays that makes Vatican politics look tame by comparison. Some of you might be thinking that Apple has no choice but to live with the airing of its dirty laundry because the story of Steve Jobs' roller coaster rides at the company is so well known. Well, think again.

We made a quick survey of the publicly disgraced and found that not everyone is quite so forthcoming. Here's an excerpt from Martha Stewart's version of the Martha Stewart story, for example:

> While earning a bachelor's degree in history and architectural history at Barnard College, Martha worked as a model to pay her tuition. She was married in her sophomore year, and upon graduating became a successful stockbroker on Wall Street, where she gained her early business training. After moving to Westport, Connecticut, in 1972 with her husband and daughter, Alexis, she developed a catering business that showcased her remarkable talent and originality. Her unique visual presentation of food and the elegant recipes she created for her catered events were the basis for her first book, *Entertaining,* published in 1982. One of the most beautiful and influential books ever published, *Entertaining* has become an American classic.[3]

From the excerpt on the official website, you might incorrectly guess that Martha is still happily married (she was divorced in 1990), that she still might be a stockbroker, or that the decision to start a catering business was the whim of a contented, but bored Connecticut housewife. Nowhere in the official biography is there any mention of Martha's brief excursion to jail resulting from alleged insider trading of ImClone Systems, Inc. So much for telling it like it is. But, if you don't tell it like it is, how do you tell it?

There are potentially as many ways to tell the story of a company as there are companies. Corporate storytelling isn't a matter of best approach versus worst approach; it's a matter of more-appropriate approach versus less-appropriate approach.

In our first example, we'd say Microsoft is a safer bet for the future, not because it tells a happier story, but because it has clearly done a better job of reading the zeitgeist and moving along than Apple. Based on its clever but vicious television spots featuring a spoof of Bill Gates, it seems Apple still exhibits an apparent nostalgia for the early days of Silicon Valley when ill-mannered nerds who engaged in public acts of defiance to anything that looked like authority were the fair-haired boys and girls of the personal computing revolution.

A Cola Ain't a Cola, Ain't a Cola

Studying the differences in the Microsoft and Apple stories got us thinking about other corporate rivalries between companies with very similar beginnings, such as Coca-Cola and Pepsi-Cola, both of which were "born" in southern pharmacies in the nineteenth century. Go to the PepsiCo website and you'll find the following inspirational story of the development of the company:

> 1902: The instant popularity of this new drink leads Bradham to devote all of his energy to developing Pepsi-Cola into a full-fledged business, and he applies for a trademark with the U.S. Patent Office in Washington, D.C. The first Pepsi-Cola Company is formed.

> 1898: One of Bradham's formulations, known as "Brad's Drink," a combination of carbonated water, sugar, vanilla, rare oils, and kola nuts, is renamed "Pepsi-Cola" on Aug. 28.

1893: Caleb Bradham, a young pharmacist from New Bern, North Carolina, begins experimenting with many different soft drink concoctions; patrons and friends sample them at his drug store fountain.[4]

Now, let's look at the Coca-Cola version:

The product that has given the world its best-known taste was born in Atlanta, Georgia, on May 8, 1886. Dr. John Stith Pemberton, a local pharmacist, produced the syrup for Coca-Cola, and carried a jug of the new product down the street to Jacobs' Pharmacy, where it was sampled, pronounced "excellent" and placed on sale for five cents a glass as a soda fountain drink. Carbonated water was teamed with the new syrup to produce a drink that was at once "Delicious and Refreshing," a theme that continues to echo today wherever Coca-Cola is enjoyed.

Thinking that "the two Cs would look well in advertising," Dr. Pemberton's partner and bookkeeper, Frank M. Robinson, suggested the name and penned the now famous trademark "Coca-Cola" in his unique script. The first newspaper ad for Coca-Cola soon appeared in the *Atlanta Journal*, inviting thirsty citizens to try "the new and popular soda fountain drink." Hand-painted oilcloth signs reading "Coca-Cola" appeared on store awnings, with the suggestion "Drink" added to inform passersby that the new beverage was for soda fountain refreshment. During the first year, sales averaged a modest nine drinks per day.

Dr. Pemberton never realized the potential of the beverage he created. He gradually sold portions of his business to various partners and, just prior to his death in 1888, sold his remaining interest in Coca-Cola to Asa G. Candler. An Atlantan with great business acumen, Mr. Candler proceeded to buy additional rights and acquire complete control.[5]

What this little comparison tells us is that Coca-Cola knows how to tell a better story. Why is it better? For one thing, thanks to details and adjectives, it just reads better. It's told as a story rather than as a series of bullet points that seems to have wandered away from a PowerPoint presentation. The message here is that if you're going to tell your story, tell it as a story. The other thing is that the Pepsi-Cola story is a story of fact, whereas the Coca-Cola story is a story about people (or more correctly, a person, because the character of Asa Candler is better developed than that of Dr. Pemberton). Coca-Cola has formally embraced corporate storytelling as one of the ways to build its brand. At the risk of stealing the thunder from our discussion of brands, we include this snippet from the company's website:

> Coca-Cola touches the lives of millions of people each and every day. From special occasions to exceptional moments in everyday life, Coca-Cola is there. The brand has become a special part of people's lives.
>
> Over the years, hundreds of people have sent us stories about how Coca-Cola has affected their lives. Whether it is a childhood memory, a reminder of family gatherings, or a recollection of good times with friends, Coca-Cola has impacted the lives of people all over the world.
>
> The following are just some of the stories people have told us about the special role Coca-Cola has played in their lives.
>
> To read the stories, click one of the links below or select a category from the menu on the left and click "go."
>
> If you would like to submit your own Coca-Cola story, select the link to the left and follow the instructions. We look forward to hearing about how Coca-Cola has played a part in your life.
>
> Romance
> Military

Reminders of Family
Special Family Times
Childhood Memories
An Affordable Luxury
Times with Friends
A Memory of Home
Coca-Cola Bottles
Coca-Cola Collectibles
Coca-Cola Employees
Advertising Stories
New Coke Stories
Bottling Companies
More Stories[6]

Not only does Coca-Cola include the consumer in its story, it provides 15 thought-starters to "remind" visitors to its website about ways they can link their memories to the brand. How successful is it? Just go to the website, click on the links, and see for yourself.

In putting together this chapter, we've opted to share and analyze a few of the ways a variety of companies in a variety of industries chose to tell their stories. Again, we need to be explicitly clear here—we aren't saying that these are the best ways to explain who you are as a corporation, but they do address some interesting challenges of corporate communications.

Martha Stewart going to jail because she took a phone call from a friend is—in the greater scheme of things—hardly a criminal cause celebré. But what story would you choose to tell if your corporation had a real checkered past, say one involving the use of slave labor?

A Tale of Two Tales

Today, ThyssenKrupp AG is a respected German industrial powerhouse. Headquartered in Düsseldorf, the firm is engaged in steel production, automotive parts production, various technologies, the elevator industry, and a variety of materials and industrial services businesses and has annual sales of € 42.1 billion and employs 184,000 people. But over half a century ago, in the midst of the Second World War, the ThyssenKrupp story was much different. During those years, the company, like all German industrial concerns, found itself operating in service to Adolf Hitler and his war machine. Describing the war effort of August Thyssen-Hütte AG, as the company was known before its merger with Fried. Krupp AG Hoesch-Krupp, the company history states the following:

> The rearmament policy pursued from the mid-1930s initially has little effect on August Thyssen-Hütte AG, which has been assigned responsibility for semi-finished products within Vereinigte Stahlwerke AG. This changes with the outbreak of war: In the regulated war economy production becomes increasingly difficult in the face of shortages of construction materials, raw materials, labor, and energy. The labor shortage caused by the conscription of employees combined with increasing arms requirements is offset by the use of foreign labor and prisoners of war.[7]

But continue reading through the corporate history, and you'll find the following note that makes the reference to "the use of foreign labor and prisoners of war" far more disturbing:

> Alfried von Bohlen und Halbach, the eldest son of Gustav (1870–1950) and Bertha (1886–1957) Krupp von Bohlen und Halbach, attends grammar school before undergoing practical training in various workshops of Fried. Krupp AG. Having studied metallurgy at the technical universities of Munich, Berlin, and Aachen, he graduates as "Diplomingenieur" in 1934 with a thesis on the melting of steel in a vacuum. After completing his training at Dresdner Bank in Berlin, he joins the family firm in 1936.

On October 1, 1938, he is appointed to the board of directors (executive board) of Fried. Krupp AG. As the designated successor to his father he is soon invited to join supervisory boards of other companies and industrial organizations. In early 1941, for instance, he is one of the founding fathers of the Imperial Coal Association and is made vice chairman of the Imperial Iron Association established in 1942. In March 1943, Alfried von Bohlen und Halbach is appointed chairman of the board of directors. On the conversion of Fried. Krupp AG into a sole proprietorship at the end of 1943, he becomes the exclusive owner of the company and also acquires the right to call himself Krupp von Bohlen und Halbach.

Alfried Krupp von Bohlen und Halbach takes over the company at a time when there is little room for independent business decisions—especially in the munitions industry. The state munitions authorities and an increasing number of semi-private control bodies regularly intervene in production planning. From a sense of duty and loyalty, he endeavors to meet the demands placed on him, despite the increasingly difficult overall situation toward the end of the war.

At the start of the American occupation, Alfried Krupp von Bohlen und Halbach is placed under automatic arrest on April 11, 1945. His property is confiscated, and he is detained in custody until 1947 when together with eleven of his senior staff he is brought before an American military tribunal in one of the three Nuremberg industrial trials. He stands accused of the same crimes originally brought against his father Gustav Krupp von Bohlen und Halbach—crimes against peace and consequent conspiracy. On these charges all the accused are found not guilty.

However, on the two other charges of plundering assets in occupied foreign countries and slave labor (crimes against humanity through the employment of foreign forced laborers and prisoners of war) Alfried Krupp von Bohlen und Halbach is sentenced to twelve years' imprisonment and all his property is confiscated. Sentences of up to twelve years are handed down to ten of those who stand trial with him. As part of a general amnesty, the then high commissioner of the American zone of Germany, John J. McCloy, grants the prisoners an early release in January 1951.[8]

What was an underplayed answer to a labor shortage in one telling becomes a crime against humanity in another. The ThyssenKrupp story provides a fascinating example of corporate mythologizing because, like the story of the creation of Eve in the Old Testament, it leaves us with not one but two explanations of what happened.

One lesson to be drawn from this is that a good story can—and in fact should—contain elements of the truth, but that, depending on the telling, some of those elements may appear to contradict each other. The other lesson is that stories, like history, are written by the survivors. In the case of ThyssenKrupp, Alfried Krupp von Bohlen und Halbach, the Krupp in the story, is the one who collaborated with the Nazis, whereas as we are about to see from this additional excerpt from the company's official history, the role of the Thyssen family is portrayed a tad differently:

August Thyssen's eldest son Fritz did not wish to become chief executive of Vereinigte Stahlwerke AG when it was founded. Instead, as the biggest single private shareholder (26%) he is elected chairman of the supervisory board. On May 1, 1933, he joins the NSDAP with great hopes of organizing the party's economic policy along corporatist lines. However, these ideas are soon no longer in line with those of the party. After the state murders committed in the so-called Röhm putsch Fritz Thyssen distances himself more and more from the NSDAP and its aims, even if Vereinigte Stahlwerke AG continues to play an important role in the Nazi's autarky and armaments economy. He does not leave the NSDAP or the Reichstag but shows his rejection of the regime through small gestures (borrowing from the "Jewish" banker Simon Hirschland, Essen; financial support for the family of the imprisoned Martin Niemöller, etc.). He breaks openly with the regime after the German attack on Poland.

In an open telegram to Hermann Göring, Fritz Thyssen refuses to appear at a Reichstag session in Berlin on September 1, 1939 to ratify the German invasion of Poland. Pushed by his family, he flees with them first to Switzerland, later to France. There he is overtaken by the events of the war and is unable to emigrate to Argentina as planned. Unoccupied Vichy France hands him and his wife Amélie over to the German Reich at the end of 1940. The state confiscates his assets, thus gaining control over the business policy of Vereinigte Stahlwerke AG.[9]

The truth is that Fritz Thyssen was a rabid anticommunist who was a major financial backer of Hitler in his drive for the German chancellorship. He did in fact leave Germany in 1939, and Hitler did confiscate his holdings. Following his repatriation, he was held in a series of camps—including Dachau—and after the war he paid a penalty equal to about 15 percent of his holdings in restitution for his early support of the Nazis.

So, we ask you, is this a case study in personal redemption or inexcusable corporate social exploitation or both? Unlike Martha Stewart's offenses, war crimes are just a little too much to sweep under even the widest corporate carpet. By acknowledging them and placing them in a specific context, ThyssenKrupp manages to position itself if not exactly as the victim of history, then as one of its survivors.

Value and Values

Of course, the odds are that your corporate story doesn't have to detour around a past that includes war crimes, making telling your story a good deal easier. Many companies choose to tell their stories using the familiar language of social cliché. In the case of Clorox, for instance, luck, pluck, and old-fashioned honesty characterize the company's story. Here's how the company tells it:

> **On May 3, 1913,** five California entrepreneurs invested $100 apiece to set up America's first commercial-scale liquid bleach factory, which they located in Oakland, on the east side of San Francisco Bay. In 1914, they named their product Clorox bleach.
>
> They were an unlikely group to embark on such an enterprise: a banker; a purveyor of wood and coal; a bookkeeper; a lawyer; and a miner, the only one of the five with any practical knowledge of chemistry.[10]

Now, if you think about it for a minute, what's so unusual about having a lawyer, a banker, an accountant, and a couple of entrepreneurs present at the birth of a new enterprise? Nothing! The Horatio Alger approach continues, however:

> On the eve of World War II, Mr. Murray—who had served as company president since 1929—died suddenly. His successor, William J. Roth, had originally been hired as a youthful "jack-of-all-trades" on the recommendation of Mrs. Murray, whose favor he had won by delivering newspapers to her store promptly each day. Once again, her instinct would prove fateful to the company's future.
>
> Extraordinary difficulties loomed for Clorox when Mr. Roth took over. Yet upon his retirement in 1957, annual sales had multiplied more than tenfold, to over $40 million. A major factor was the customer and supplier loyalty nurtured by Mr. Roth's wartime business practices.

Although chlorine was in short supply, Clorox, unlike many competitors, curtailed production rather than dilute its product.

Mr. Roth, meanwhile, had also torn up pre-war contracts that would have enabled Clorox to purchase scarce chlorine at prices unfair to suppliers. The consequent cuts in production to maintain the bleach at full strength and the expenses of paying suppliers the going rate proved costly in the short run. But Clorox emerged from the war with a reservoir of good will and high public regard for the consistent quality of its bleach.[11]

A rather self-effacing history for a corporate colossus that has done a more-than-effective job of fending off direct competition for more than 90 years. The story of counterculture ice cream maker Ben & Jerry's is, like the Microsoft and Apple stories, a "buddy story" and, like Clorox, a story of the importance of combining personal values with business practices.[12]

Ben Cohen and Jerry Greenfield first met in a seventh-grade gym class in Merrick, New York. Fourteen years later, the friends moved to Vermont, where, with a $12,000 investment, they opened their first ice cream store. The balance of the story paints a picture of two lucky, music and sugar-loving hippies having a great time and trying to save the world in the process. There's "Free Cone Day," the establishment of the Ben & Jerry's Foundation, the launching of the "Cowmobile," the introduction of the first ice cream named for a rock star (Cherry Garcia), "1% for Peace," protests of the Seabrook nuclear power plant, and so on.

Only 8 lines of the 11-page corporate history are devoted to the company's acquisition in 2000 by Unilever, hardly the first corporate name you'd associate with tie-dying, social protest, and folk festivals. The official history puts it this way:

[April 12, 2000] Ben & Jerry's announces the company's acquisition by Anglo-Dutch corporation, Unilever. Ben &

Jerry's Board of Directors approve Unilever's offer of $326 million ($43.60 per share, for 8.4 million outstanding shares), as well as a unique agreement enabling Ben & Jerry's to join forces with Unilever to create an even more dynamic, socially positive ice cream business with a much more global reach.[13]

We're not so sure that's how the Unilever side of the acquisition saw it, but again, stories are told by the survivors.

Choosing the Right Corporate Story

As we said earlier in this chapter, when it comes to telling the story of the corporation, appropriate and inappropriate are much better guideposts than right and wrong. You have to find a story that fits you and tell it in a way that makes sense within the context of what people think of you.

Although it isn't the best effort we've seen, Ben and Jerry's approach fits their perceived corporate culture better than something like, "On April 12, 2000, Ben and Jerry's was purchased and became one more in a series of ice cream brands owned by a foreign global conglomerate."

By the way, speaking of corporate stories, Unilever's is pretty well done and ties well to its current mission:

In the 1890s, William Hesketh Lever, founder of Lever Bros, wrote down his ideas for Sunlight Soap—his revolutionary new product that helped popularize cleanliness and hygiene in Victorian England. It was 'to make cleanliness commonplace; to lessen work for women; to foster health and contribute to personal attractiveness, that life may be more enjoyable and rewarding for the people who use our products.'

This was long before the phrase "Corporate Mission" had been invented, but these ideas have stayed at the heart of our business. Even if their language—and the notion of only women doing housework—has become outdated.

In a history that now crosses three centuries, Unilever's success has been influenced by the major events of the day—economic boom, depression, world wars, changing consumer lifestyles, and advances in technology. And throughout we've created products that help people get more out of life—cutting the time spent on household chores, improving nutrition, enabling people to enjoy food and take care of their homes, their clothes, and themselves.[14]

Although there are no hard-and-fast rules for telling your corporate story, here are 11 basic suggestions:

1. Try to make your story as human as possible. Make it the story of people, and let their human faces become the face of the company. William Lever trying to make Victorians cleaner is a more-endearing image than the balance sheet of a multinational.

2. Tell your story—not your story you wish you had. It's alright to be aspirational about the future, but it's dangerous to be aspirational about the past.

3. It's a story—feel free to make it colorful.

4. If you're stuck for a plot, consult the classics. The annals of mythology and folklore are full of good plot lines and literary devices. One of them is bound to fit.

5. Whenever possible, let your customers help tell your story for you. Nothing is more authentic than the voice of the economically disinterested.

6. Remember you're telling this story to an audience that either (a) hasn't heard it, (b) doesn't know the players involved, (c) doesn't really care about it until you give them a reason to care, (d) is skeptical, (e) is flat out hostile to you, or (f) any or all of the above.

7. Keep your story refreshed. History is fine, but not at the expense of contemporary touch points.

8. Be conscious of opportunities to tie your vision statement and related corporate declarations (mission statement, corporate credo, web materials, press releases, and so on) to your story. The Unilever story is in reality an argument for go-to-market continuity over time.

9. Don't get so carried away embellishing your story that it becomes a target for your critics. Your words can always be turned against you if you aren't careful.

10. Like any good storyteller, remain constantly aware of the audience—always remember who they are and how they prefer to be addressed. And never forget that your corporate audience is both internal and external, including employees, potential investors, analysts (if you're publicly held or thinking about it), the media, your competition, your current and potential customers, people you might want to hire, and on a bad day, the government.

11. Finally, if you're not comfortable telling your own story, hire someone to tell it for you.. There are lots of storytellers around, from *good* public relations and marketing firms to professional authors. But make sure that whomever you hire has the tools needed to effectively frame your story and enough passion for it that they approach it as more than an academic exercise or routine fee-for-service assignment.

As you'll see in the next chapter, many of these same rules can be applied to telling the story of your brands.

hese were sad and troubled days for the giants. Physically towering over the world of mortal men had proved an evolutionary disadvantage for the Titans of brand management and marketing. True, their height allowed them to see farther than any other creature in the universe. But their vision was so powerful it all but compelled them to focus on vast horizons where ideas danced like fairies bathed in moonlight. Try as they might, they were victims of their own nature, just too big to see the world of men in clear enough detail.

This limitation caused the Titans great unhappiness. All they wanted was to make people happy. Hadn't they given the world of men great gifts? "I always thought your flavored screwdrivers designed for workers who couldn't take a lunch break were brilliant," Hippius the Titan consoled Slickus, his brother giant.

"Oh, them?" his brother said, the faintest hint of a smile crossing his broad visage. "They were nothing compared to your pastel-wall tires! I'm sure they would have caught on if those pesky humans were a bit less critical of everything we give them."

"Our mistake was not insisting on absolute obedience in exchange for our gifts," agreed Hippius. "After all, they seemed excited enough when we gave them Mell-O the first time. They were even apparently grateful. But when it came around to all those wonderful line extensions, did they care how much hard work we had put in? Of course they didn't! Why, hardly any of them even bothered to try the Jalapeño and Wild Tibetan Goji Berry–flavored Mell-O!"

"I know, I know," Slickus said as a tear rolled down his cheek and fell to the earth, creating another lake on the surface of the world of men. "But the worst of it is that they quit listening to all my wonderful stories," said Equivocatious, the sole Titan tasked with attaching stories to his brothers' inventions. "At first they seemed to need my stories," the storytelling giant said, his voice breaking slightly. "Then they stopped needing the stories to understand our gifts, but they still seemed to enjoy them—one could almost say they enhanced the gifts a bit, if I may be so bold."

"But slowly things began to change," Equivocatious continued, his massive brow furrowing in anger. "They didn't seem to appreciate how daunting a task it is to come up with completely new stories every time there's a new gift. They began to analyze the stories and through their analysis find fault. They used those wonderful computers and the Internet we gave them to build websites to attack and mock our stories. They quarreled with the golden phrases of the ages, like 'new and improved' and 'value pack.' They even used old stories to attack new ones and vice versa. And what's it led to? They criticize us for giving them gifts. The puny little ingrates! It's no wonder I've been hitting the lotus leaves a little hard lately."

"Relax, my brother," said Coolius, one of the cleverest of all the Titans. "Have a double Grey Goose martini and set down those leaves and listen. It isn't that they've completely forgotten our stories. We can still use bits and pieces of them to get them to appreciate our gifts. It's just that they've gotten used to telling each other their own stories. All we have to do is learn how to listen to that babbling they call language and incorporate some of their words into the bits and pieces of our stories that they still revere. That way, they won't think we're talking to them at all. They'll hear their words, vaguely remember our stories, and the rest will just naturally sort itself out."

"You want us to listen to them?" challenged Hippius, Slickus, and Equivocatious with one roaring voice.

"It's the only way," said Coolius. "If we want to continue to give them gifts—which is in fact what our nature commands us to do—then we have no choice but to listen to them and tell stories they understand, using their language to do it."

Soon the Titans were lost in debate. Sensing that his brothers were hopelessly deadlocked and realizing they were falling terribly behind in their gift production, Coolius stood and demanded a moment to speak. "Fear not my brothers," he said. "We aren't giving up any of our power. Let's just call our new approach 'Alternative Marketing' and consider it as just another gift." The Titans saw the wisdom of Coolius's words. What happened next is another story.

Chapter 10

APPLIED STORYTELLING 101: THE BRAND

"Storytelling: The art of creating a compelling narrative for your product and brand that connects emotionally with your customers. Think Pixar."

—BusinessWeek online, "Buzzwords 2005: A Glossary"

"The Maori people of New Zealand talk about surrounding their great treasures with 'interesting talk.' This, they believe, increases the mana (standing) of the object. I believe this too.... Great brands have always been surrounded by great stories."

—Kevin Roberts, Lovemarks: The Future Beyond Brands

"Stories are powerful ways to vividly communicate the brand's identity and its heritage. Many are the source of legend and get passed on, while others get lost to posterity unless the organization actively packages them."

—David A. Aaker and Erich Joachimsthaler, Brand Leadership

"The basic tool for the manipulation of reality is the manipulation of words. If you can control the meaning of words, you can control the people who must use the words."

—Philip K. Dick

"Brands are the stories that unite us all in a common purpose within an enterprise, and connect us with the people we serve on the outside. These brand stories give meaning to who we are and what we do."

—Mark Thomson

A Modest Proposal on the Topic of Brands

In Chapter 5, "Who Owns Your Brand?" we took a long look at the relationship between branding and storytelling. In this chapter, we move from theory to application.

Every industry—including such late entries to the mass-marketing fray as institutional financial services and pharmaceuticals—has become much more aggressive in the branding/storytelling arena. Whether it's ING plastering its name all over park benches in commercials or those AstraZeneca ads for the "purple pill," everyone seems to be trying to crack the new branding code by finding new ways—and new arenas—to tell their stories.

Increasingly, branders are turning to "entertainment"—including storytelling—to plead their case before the public. As Louise Story observed, "Marketers have found a new way to try to keep viewers from tuning out: Urge them to tune in, by creating their own TV shows, movies, and online programming—often with help from their advertising agencies."[1] Among these new advertainment offerings, or "branded content" as they are known in the trade, are "Instant Def" from Snickers and BBDO New York (online), "Home Made Simple" from Procter & Gamble (on TLC), and "Schooled" from Office Max and DDB Chicago (ABC Family).

The Metaverse and Beyond

Many branders are pushing the frontiers even further. Eric Kintz, vice president of global marketing and excellence for HP, recently looked at the impact of "new media" on his blogsite. "New technologies have allowed consumers to disaggregate the content form the promotion," he wrote. "They are 'tuning out' from traditional advertising by migrating to new platforms (think MySpace, YouTube, and others) or by using technologies that allow them to skip advertising (DVRs, RSS feeds, pop-up blockers, etc). New technologies have also enabled a level of engagement that was not possible before—consumers are talking back and a unique opportunity is emerging for brands to engage in the dialogue."[2]

To Kintz, it is critical that the brand storyteller move to whatever digital campfire his or her audience selects. "We will follow consumers on platforms and media they value," he said. "We have already massively shifted our advertising spend toward the web. We are now also experimenting with various new media from video pre-rolls, to mobile banners that lead to mobile microsites, podcasting pre-rolls, Napster pre-rolls, or RSS sponsorships.

"We will engage in very different ways with consumers allowing more interaction (for example, through blogs) or even enabling consumers to play with our advertising campaigns. The partnership with Personiva for our Personal Again Campaign is a great example of this trend."[3]

Kintz believes the lingua franca of Internet communication is evolving from text to video and that consumers will "expect video components in their traditional search and will expect better results in their video search."

There's yet another branding frontier beyond YouTube and MySpace—a digital wilderness that its zealous pioneers refer to as the metaverse—named after a virtual world in *Snow Crash*, a cyberpunk novel by Neal Stephenson. The metaverse is an online three-dimensional universe, a life space where commerce is quickly following digital role playing and social engineering. Second Life is the north star of this new universe. At this writing, Second Life, the creation of Linden Lab, has a "population" of more than 1.1 million and is growing at about 38 percent a month. Second Life isn't alone. Mindmark's Entropria Universe has 500,000 inhabitants and is also growing rapidly.

Cynical marketers tend to gravitate to places where millions of young, affluent, early adopters gather, and the metaverse is no exception. This helps explains the explosion in discussions of "v- (for virtual world) business." Both Adidas and Reebok sell virtual shoes in Second Life, perfect for wearing when you're driving the virtual cars sold by Toyota and Nissan to the virtual hotels operated in Second Life by Starwood Hotels. Goods and services are paid for with the Linden dollars, Second Life's official currency, which trades, at par, with the U.S. dollar.

How much is it all worth? As the BBC's Jonathan Fildes reported, "Some estimates put the economic value of Second Life in 2005 at $64 million (£33 million). Meanwhile Project Entropia saw $1.6 billion pass though the world in the same year, which is set to double in 2006. Some objects, like a virtual space station commanded a price of $100,000."[4]

Second Life is rapidly attracting other kinds of firms, such as Rivers Run Red, an advertising and events company that helped organize the BBC's One Big Weekend, a virtual/physical music festival held in Dundee, Scotland. IBM has already hosted meetings in Second Life and has an employee, Roo Reynolds, whose business card reads "Metaverse Evangelist."

Commercial storytellers are scrambling to find the best ways to reach audiences who gather around dozens of new digital campfires from BlackBerrys and Q phones, to blogs and splogs, broadband and wireless applications, iPods, interactive media, and of course, a host of web-based applications. But whatever the vehicle, certain branding rules stay constant. And, if you want to tell your brand's story, you best begin by rethinking branding itself.

What Is a Brand?

Brands have been variously described as "trustmarks," "lovemarks," and even in the words of our friend, branding guru extraordinaire Scott Bedbury, "...the result of a synaptic process in the brain."[5] Brands have been burned, painted, and inked onto skins. They are registered with governments and applied (with greater and lesser success) to the roar of a Harley-Davidson engine and the use of a specific shade of pink in insulation. Analyzing, theorizing, defining, and then redefining the meaning of brands and branding has become a growing cottage industry.

Every year, a mind-numbing number of books, articles, speeches, and websites are devoted to the problem of getting "new" insights on brands—for several very practical reasons.

First, on the more venial side, brand marketers, brand managers, advertising agencies, and even the odd marketing-oriented CEO or two never seem to tire of talking to themselves and reemphasizing the importance of their mission. Come up with a new cliché to describe the process of attaching meaning to a proprietary object—tangible or virtual—and you're all but guaranteed your 15 minutes in the center ring of the peripatetic branding circus.

Second, and more important, brands and branding really matter, and not just to branders. Even in today's jaded commercial environment, a significant body of consumers still believe in brands. A great brand can float a mediocre product or indemnify a new service offering. Whether you operate in the business-to-business or business-to-consumer arena or both, nothing means as much to you—or should mean as much to you—as your brand.

We're going to avoid the obvious trap of saying something like, "A brand is a story," no matter how neatly that might dovetail into the framework of this book. The truth is—that for this exercise—we really don't care what a brand is, at least in the abstract sense. We don't think that theories of branding build brands, move products, or sell services. Sure, theories are obviously important to branders themselves, but what's really important to the branders who want to effectively communicate with their customer? Or, even more simply put, what's really important to the brander's audience? We think the answer to that question is a good story. As Douglas Rushkoff put it, "We use stories to understand our world, orient ourselves, motivate our employees, communicate our brand values, and even tout our stock valuation. So, our relationship to these stories really does matter."[6]

Let's take a quick look at the top 10 international brands for 2005, as ranked by Interbrand.[7]

Ranking	Brand	2005 Brand Value ($m)
1	Coca-Cola	67,525
2	Microsoft	59,941
3	IBM	53,376
4	GE	46,996
5	Intel	35,588
6	Nokia	26,452
7	Disney	26,441
8	McDonald's	26,014
9	Toyota	24,837
10	Marlboro	21,189

We've already devoted a good deal of attention to how Coca-Cola and some of the other companies on this list use stories and storytelling to enhance their brand, so we've opted to briefly focus on how IBM and Disney approach storytelling before we go into a more general discussion of the relationship of storytelling or myth making to brands and branding.

IBM

Visit IBM's home page on the Internet, find the History section, and you'll encounter the following introduction to the history of a great brand:

> The character of a company—the stamp it puts on its products, services, and the marketplace—is shaped and defined over time. It evolves. It deepens. It is expressed in an ever-changing corporate culture, in transformational strategies, and in new and compelling offerings for customers. IBM's character has been formed over nearly 100 years of doing business in the field of information-handling. Nearly all

of the company's products were designed and developed to record, process, communicate, store and retrieve information—from its first scales, tabulators and clocks to today's powerful computers and vast global networks.

IBM helped pioneer information technology over the years, and it stands today at the forefront of a worldwide industry that is revolutionizing the way in which enterprises, organizations and people operate and thrive.

"The pace of change in that industry, of course, is accelerating, and its scope and impact are widening. In these pages, you can trace that change from the earliest antecedents of IBM, to the most recent developments. You can scan the entire IBM continuum from the 19th century to the 21st or pinpoint—year by year or decade by decade—the key events that have led to the IBM of today. We hope that you enjoy this unique look back at the highly textured history of the International Business Machines Corporation.[8]

We could go on and on (it's a very detailed history), but we thought we'd just take one more sample, a description of the 40-year-old Thomas J. Watson, Sr., as he joined the staff of Computing-Tabulating-Recording Company as general manager:[9]

Drawing upon his sales experience at NCR, Watson implemented a series of effective business tactics: generous sales incentives, a focus on customer service, an insistence on well-groomed, dark-suited salesmen and an evangelical fervor for instilling company pride and loyalty in every worker. Watson boosted company spirit with employee sports teams, family outings and a company band. He preached a positive outlook, and his favorite slogan, "THINK," became a mantra for C-T-R's employees. Within 11 months of joining C-T-R, Watson became its president. The company focused on providing large-scale, custom-built tabulating solutions for businesses, leaving the market for small office products to others. During Watson's first four years, revenues more than doubled to $9 million. He also expanded the company's operations to Europe, South America, Asia and Australia.[10]

The apparent story of the man is also a cleverly constructed story of the company, which, in this case, is also the story of the brand. Note the careful use of language. Business tactics are *effective.* Sales incentives are *generous.* There is a *focus* on customer service. Morale is *boosted,* and outlooks are *positive.* Business solutions are *large scale* and *custom built.*

Now return to the introduction to the history. The company has a character that is *shaped and defined over time* and which *evolves and deepens.* The corporate culture is *ever-changing,* strategies are *transformational,* and offerings are *new and compelling.* And remember, this isn't the selling part of the site. Or is it?

Of course, there are some bumps along the road. The only line in the history dealing with IBM's loss of control of the interface for the personal computer comes as a tagline on a paragraph about the first IBM PC: "The processor chip came from Intel and the operating system, called DOS (Disk Operating System) came from a 32-person company called Microsoft."[11]

All in all—and a bit of corporate face-saving aside—it's not a bad way to tell the story of the company and the brand.

Disney

You don't need us to tell you that the Disney organization understands stories better than almost any corporation on Earth. Stories are, after all, the patina that covers almost every Disney product. Even the language of Disney reflects this emphasis on stories and storytelling. Employees at the parks are referred to as "cast members," suggesting they're playing out roles in a living theater. When you think Disney, you're supposed to think happy thoughts.

Oddly, a visit to the Disney Online website, "The Official Home Page of The Walt Disney Company," openly discusses the darker side of Walt Disney, a man whose name has become a synonymy for everything wholesome. It discusses his inability to manage money well, for example, as well as his lack of trust in people, which followed a bitter strike against his studio in 1941. It also addresses more sensitive topics, including allegations that Walt Disney was anti-Semitic:

> Did Walt make offhand comments about the Jewish union members during the painful strike of 1940? Likely. Might some of his executives have harbored anti-Semitic feelings that were wrongly ascribed to Walt himself? Very possibly. Did some of his early cartoons—notably "Three Little Pigs"—contain the kind of unpleasant Jewish caricatures that were common to many cartoon studios at the time? Certainly. Did a few Jewish men who had difficult relationships with Walt speculate that the reason was because they were Jewish? Also yes.[12]

The official history clears Disney of these allegations, offering up as evidence the fact that its authors are themselves Jewish and they had found no proof of anti-Semitic behavior. Disney's distrust of unions is handled in a similar manner:

> Of course, the great formative experience in Walt's political life was the strike against the Studio in 1941. Walt became firmly convinced that many of the strike's leaders were Communist-sympathizing men and women whose interest was more in advancing a political ideology than genuinely helping the workers. Is that true? The passage of time has made it difficult to know. However, it is clear that this belief stiffened his resolve, to make sure that Communists did not gain a foothold in Hollywood or elsewhere in the United States. With that in mind, he took some actions that in retrospect leave him vulnerable to criticism. In 1944, for example, Walt helped to found a conservative organization

called the Motion Picture Alliance for the Preservation of American Ideas. One of the goals of the organization was to fight "Communists, radicals, and crackpots."

When Walt was called upon to testify before the House Un-American Activities Committee, he did so willingly. The majority of his testimony dealt with his feelings that the strike had been manipulated by Communists. He testified that the Communists "smeared me.... They distorted everything, they lied; ...they formed picket lines in front of the theaters and, well, they called my plant a sweatshop, and that is not true, and anybody in Hollywood would prove it otherwise."

When he was asked about his personal opinion of the Communist Party, Walt replied, "Well, I don't believe it is a political party. I believe it is an un-American thing. The thing that I resent the most is that they are able to get into these unions, take them over, and represent to the world that a group of people that are in my plant, that I know are good, 100 percent Americans, are trapped by this group and they are represented to the world as support[ing] all of those ideologies, and it is not so, and I feel that they really ought to be smoked out and shown up for what they are, so that all of the good, free causes in this country, all the liberalisms that really are American, can go out without the taint of Communism."[13]

Visitors to the website learn not only that Disney (who eventually died of lung cancer) smoked but that he liked a cocktail now and again:

The general public was virtually unaware that Walt smoked at all. Out of thousands of photographs published of him during his lifetime, virtually none show him smoking; artful cropping at the studio ensured that. Walt also enjoyed a drink or two at the end of the day. For years, his drink of choice was an Irish Mist—a mixture of scotch and crushed ice. But he rarely drank during the workday. Though he didn't approve of staffers who had liquid lunches—and given the pressure of the Studio, there were more than one—he rarely brought the matter up. All that mattered was that they got their work done. In the late 1960s he told Imagineer Marty Sklar, "You know something? I'm not Walt Disney anymore. Walt Disney is a thing. An image that people have in their minds. And I spent my whole life building this. Walt Disney isn't that image. I smoke and I drink and there's a whole lot of other things that I do that I don't want to be part of that image." This may have been a major tactical error on Walt's part— as well as the publicists' at the studio. By perpetuating a mythic, idealized version of the man—the so-called "Disney Version," as author Richard Schickel put it in his less-than-positive portrait of Walt—they opened the door to countless revisionist versions of his life. There are some journalists—some good, some bad—who regard any previously hidden information as a sure sign that there are closets full of skeletons, ready to be exposed to a world that enjoys seeing its great men and women defiled.[14]

It's interesting to note that even the master storyteller himself was, in the end, overtaken by the story he had so artfully crafted and told to the public. Paradoxically, the storytellers who followed him seemed to have learned the lesson Disney himself hadn't. By presenting a more-rounded version of the man—albeit with all the sharp edges ground down to safety by explanation and sympathetic observation—they begin to close those doors to revisionism, if ever so slightly. One of the oddest admissions in the history is that maybe Walt wanted to pursue less than PG-rated projects:

In fact, in his last years Walt sometimes gave vent to the thought that he was a not entirely happy prisoner of the image he had created. When parents sipped martinis in *The Parent Trap* and a prostitute bantered with Fred MacMurray in *Bon Voyage,* he was beset with complaints. Of the '*Bon Voyage* scene, he later said, "That was a disaster. You should have seen the mail I got over it. I'll never do that again." "He was concerned and frustrated by the fact that he couldn't do something a little off-color," said Ron Miller. "But he had created this image. I'll never forget, when he saw the movie *To Kill a Mockingbird,* he said, 'It's too bad I can't make a picture like that....' He was locked in a corner." In fact, this frustration moved him to spend less time in the studio and more and more time with WED, a company that Walt started with his own money to work on Disneyland.[15]

Clearly, a more human Disney is a more sympathetic—and by extension less attackable—Disney. Here we have an unapologetic smoker who dies of lung cancer; a family-oriented guy who enjoyed a few quick belts; a man who, at one point in his career, employed popular anti-Semitic imagery but was ostensibly the soul of religious liberalism; a union-hating fanatic whose views on organized labor alienated him from those who worked for him and led him to see Communists behind every picket sign; and a moviemaker who wanted to have the freedom to do a little "blue" material if he wanted to. He is, to borrow a phrase from Nietzsche, "Human, all too human." Hey, it's a good story, and they're sticking to it.

Disney provides us with a great example of defensive story-telling or revisionist mythology. The man became both a brand and the reification of the company. As long as the man was subject to attack, so was the brand. The story of the man has to diverge at some point from the story of the brand, a maneuver that, when correctly executed, simultaneously preserves the brand and makes the man look flawed but somehow more accessible and therefore more human. It's a strategy that worked for years for brand Disney and more recently was successfully mimicked by brand Martha Stewart.

There's nothing accidental in the way the official Disney history reinforces and indemnifies the Disney brand. We hope the same can be said for how you preserve and nurture your brand story. What is the lesson for storytellers here? Stories are enhanced by friction, but they can't tolerate inherent major conflict. The reason the lessons of classic mythology have come down to us essentially unchanged is that the storylines are easy to follow. Characters stay in character. Conflicts emerge, build to a pitch, and are resolved. Fickle, monomaniacal gods don't suddenly turn democratic and consistent. Heroes may have moments of weakness, but they remain heroes throughout the story.

The mythology of branding operates on the same principles. Brands can't tolerate significant, irreconcilable internal conflicts. Conflicts can be tolerated as long as they don't touch the essence or primary activity associated with the brand. We don't mind Walt Disney's little flaws because they don't distract from the essential nature of his character—the visionary artist dedicated to celebrating the virtue of creative imagination and making its fruits tangible, safe, and fun for a family. So what if Walt had his moments? Aren't all artists supposed to be a little bit odd? The Disney brand survives the apparent conflict—between alleged anti-Semitism, drinking, smoking, and wholesome family fun—precisely because of the overriding brand attributes—art, imagination, and creativity. The uncreative assume all artists are a little eccentric and so character flaws——even major ones like anti-Semitism—are either glossed over or ignored completely. In some perverse sense, in the case of Disney, they actually enhance the brand's image——after all, the more creative, the more eccentric.

The same holds true for Martha Stewart. So what if she did a little insider trading? Isn't part of the public's fascination with her that she is a powerful businesswoman who moves in circles most of her fans could never even aspire to? And aren't the rules governing those circles different from those that regulate mere mortals? Not to mention that Martha's "core story" is the tale of a woman who, armed only with a serving spoon, can take a gourd she grew in her own organic garden and make a chandelier out of it in less than 45 seconds. Being able to cook and make holiday decorations is a separate activity from investment. We don't care about that side of Martha's life. As long as she's making wild dandelion salad and losing the cell-decorating contest, she's got our attention, and apparently our support.

We routinely forgive people who step completely out of character (that is, whose behavior has little to do with the core attributes that attract us to their story). Bill Clinton's sexual indiscretions might not have endeared him to conservatives—or monogamists—but his critics failed to bring him down. Why not? Well, because, as much as we're drawn to political sex scandals as a nation, we apparently don't see personal sexual behavior as a critical part of the story of national governance. Clinton's detractors thought that a leader's moral character was a key element in telling a political story. They clearly hadn't paid much attention to the history of politics. Scandal, or rumors of scandal, have been attached to any number of presidents, including Andrew Jackson, Warren Harding, John F. Kennedy, and even Dwight Eisenhower. Had Clinton proved himself a less effective leader, the story might have had a far different ending.

Now contrast the Clinton story with that of Bernie Ebbers. Or remember the scramble of political leaders, including President Bush, to distance themselves from the affairs of political lobbyist Jack Abramoff, an example of a story whose central theme was individual ethical character. The same kinds of sins we routinely excuse in some celebrities (ruthlessness, egomania, greed, duplicity) become the focal point of the story. Bernie Ebbers is just as greedy and arrogant as Donald Trump, but Trump's greed and arrogance have made him a media star. Where we expect—in fact demand—Trump to behave "badly," we punish Ebbers and other corporate leaders when they exhibit similar personality characteristics or behaviors. Ethics is clearly not an attribute we expect in the stories of celebrities, but it is one we look for in business leaders.

SLAM!

Let's look at one more—perhaps somewhat unorthodox—example before we explore a set of general rules for the uses of storytelling in branding. We've selected World Wrestling Entertainment, Inc. (WWE) for several reasons. For one thing, although total revenue (North America and International) has drifted slightly downward from $374.3 million in 2003 to $366.4 million in 2005, net income from continuing operations during the same period jumped from $16.1 million to $37.8 million. Not too bad given the fickleness of the entertainment market, especially when you remember we're talking about professional wrestling. Even more important, WWE is a great example of a company that has consciously chosen to build its brand on the effective use of storytelling.

Explaining its business strategy on its corporate website, the company states:

> Our formula is straightforward. We develop compelling storylines anchored by our Superstars. This content drives television ratings, which, in turn, drive pay-per-view buys, live event attendance and branded merchandise sales. Our strategy is to capitalize on the significant operating leverage of our business model through the distribution of this intellectual property across existing platforms, as well as new and emerging distribution platforms.[16]

WWE explains its brand strategy this way:

> *Continue to strengthen our brands.* In spring 2002, we made the strategic decision to separate our content into two brands, RAW and SmackDown! By having two brands, we are able to more effectively expand our fan base and establish stronger brand loyalty. The creation of dual brands with distinct storylines, tours and talent has allowed us to expand our touring schedule, particularly outside North America.[17]

Admittedly, following the WWE plots requires a bit less erudition than, say, reading *Finnegans Wake* or finding a cure for cancer, but near universal, lowest common denominator appeal is the true beauty of the brand. By the way, the stories used to sell the brand are as old as time: good versus evil, the hero's journey, the fall and redemption, lovers' triangles, greed versus virtue, and so on.

To make it even easier to follow, WWE's pantheon of heroes and villains is neatly divided into two groups: RAW Superstars and SmackDown Superstars, many of whom post names borrowed directly from pop culture (particularly movies), politics, and other mass-market touchstones. Among the RAW talent, we find Carlito (as in the Al Pacino movie), Edge (as in U2's guitarist), Kane (as in Abel), Romeo (as in Juliet), Stone Cold (as in the Brian Bosworth movie), and The Rock (as in Gibraltar). The SmackDown crew includes Batista (as in the former Cuban dictator), Boogeyman (as in don't let him get you), Booker T (as in Washington or the MGs, we're not really sure), the Undertaker (enough said; who was initially "managed" by Paul Bearer [enough said]), Super Crazy (ditto), and Road Warrior-Animal (as in the Mel Gibson movie).

Those who denounce professional wrestling as cartoons with human actors both get and miss the point. Cartoons and wrestling are anchored by easily identifiable (one could say stereotypical) characters and equally recognizable plots. Each genre represents a pop-culture iteration of the themes of classical mythology and folklore. Fans are drawn to them not because they can't wait to see what happens but because they know exactly what is going to happen. Even when there is an apparent role switch (as when "hero" Hulk Hogan suddenly became villain Hollywood Hulk Hogan, member of the evil New World Order), the fans know the hero had just temporarily lost his way during his journey to truth and self-knowledge.

Stop us if this story seems a bit familiar. The Undertaker's existence is clouded by a homicidal relationship to his half-brother, Kane (who else?). Here's how the official WWE Superstar Profile explains Kane's entrance into the world of professional wrestling:

> Following months of speculation, Kane made his first appearance on Oct. 5, 1997, at Bad Blood. There, he ripped the cage door off during the first-ever Hell in a Cell Match between Shawn Michaels and Undertaker. Kane and Undertaker then stood toe to toe during a chilling staredown. The Big Red Monster (Kane) wore a mask, and he hid his body in attire designed to conceal hideous burns from a fire supposedly started by his half-brother, Undertaker. Then, Kane kicked the Deadman in the stomach and Tombstoned him—allowing a bloody Michaels to pin Undertaker for the victory.
>
> Despite the unprovoked attack, Undertaker vowed he would not wage war against his own flesh and blood in front of a national audience. But Kane's assaults continued, and when he set Undertaker ablaze inside a casket at the 1998 Royal Rumble, the Phenom *(the Undertaker for the uninitiated)* was left with no choice. At WrestleMania XIV, the half-brothers met for the first time in singles competition, but it was only the beginning.[18]

In other words, WWE cofounder, chairman of the board of directors, and chairman of the executive committee, Vincent K. McMahon, also the cofounder of World Wrestling Entertainment, Inc., has gone the Bible one better: The homicidal sibling rivalry between the twenty-first-century Kane and his brother isn't over until the script—based on fan reaction—says it's over. McMahon not only knows his icons—the Undertaker began this incarnation of his pro wrestling career as a sort of a zombified version of an Old West mortician—but he also knows how to mix his metaphors and weave them into a classical story line.

Tools for Storytelling Brand Builders

It's probably worth noting that all the rules associated with using stories to build companies can also be applied to the brands they produce. After all, on one level, it's all about storytelling, whether it's the story of an industry, a company, a brand, or even an individual product. Branding, however, is clearly a separate activity from corporate marketing or positioning. As we've seen, "Brand Disney" did define the Disney organization, its products, and even its creator, but the successful use of storytelling to support brands requires some subtle nuances.

So, here are our 10 rules for storytelling branders:

1. Brands are the tangible connection points between an enterprise and its customers. A brand's story must engage an audience at a human level to be effective, which is why customer testimonials and the more recent idea of customer brand codevelopment are so critical. There's a reason why champion athletes say, "I'm going to Disneyland," instead of "Go to Disneyland." Marketers like to think of a brand's abstract values. But people purchase goods and services, not abstract concepts.

2. Stick to basic plots. Branding is essentially an exercise in democratic communication, so keep your brand plots simple and classical. Complex plots are all right in novels and foreign films, but they don't play well when it comes to brands. Branding isn't a game of subtlety, so brand stories should be built with interlocking layers of nuance.

3. Remember, you're telling a story. Good stories entertain; great stories allow people to discover themselves or some hitherto hidden aspect of themselves. Great brands like Coke and Disney encourage people to make their own connections with a product or service offering.

4. Avoid mixed messaging. It might seem obvious, but simple stories never involve contradictory elements. Even in the

case of the WWE, where some characters seem to shift from good or bad, there is a significant use of "back story" and commentary to explain the apparent shifts in behavior.

5. Speaking of characters, the development of "great" characters is one of the elements that set good stories apart. Brands that have developed iconic characters—from Charmin's Mr. Whipple, to the Energizer bunny, to Mr. Clean, the Jolly Green Giant, and all their cartoon peers—tend to have messaging that we retain longer, sometimes even after the brand support communication or the brands themselves have been cancelled. But, as we learned from Afleck, sometimes characters can grow so large that your story can no longer contain them.

6. Brands are statements of values, so branding stories need to be more like fables than fairy tales. In others words, branding stories are most effective when they have a moral or ethical underpinning, as in the case of the Working Assets credit card or Starbuck's Ethos water, where a certain percentage of profit is donated to good causes. If you want people to believe in your brand, the first step is to tell them what the brand itself believes in.

7. The time horizon of your branding story needs to be tied to the characteristics of your brand. If your brand stays static over time, your stories should be tied to tradition and rooted in history, as in the Kellogg commercials that tell adults it's all right for them to enjoy the same cereals they did as children. On the other hand, if your brands are more dynamic and innovative—as in the case of high-technology or communication-technology products—you need to stress that any story is just a chapter and not the entire book.

8. All stories need to be entertaining, and brand stories are no different.

9. In the same way that brands are statements of values, they are also statements of qualities or characteristics. We can't emphasize enough how important understanding your audience and understanding your audience's understanding of the brand is to successful brand storytelling. Let's take Volvo, for example. Most audiences understand that the story of Volvo is the story of safety. Trying to introduce a high-speed, pure sports car into the Volvo story would be like introducing a value-priced Lamborghini; it just wouldn't fit. The successful understanding of brand storytelling rests on recognizing the limitations of what we'll call—for lack of a better term—the breadth of your brand story.

10. Finally, while conflict is a critical element in most story-telling, it needs to be tightly controlled in branding situations. When Avis told its "We try harder" story, it was also telling the audience it wasn't the number one brand. In the same way, local retailers who try to tell the story of the value of hometown tradition in the face of a Wal-Mart market entry often end up sounding like they need protection from a competitor who can't be bested in a fair fight. David and Goliath is a good story, but not when David ends up looking like a whining, price-gouging schemer and Goliath comes off as a gentle giant trying to bring bounty to the land.

"*Come in. Come in. Come in,*" sputtered the fidgety man in the faun-colored faux-Armani suit. "Welcome to Custom Tales, my most modest empo-rium. Aldous Loki, as in 'Low Key,' at your service. No pressure here. No hard sell. No sir. At Custom Tales, we have everything for individuals who in—er, forgive me—midlife find their stories in need of, well, let's just say a bit of rework. In many cases, all that's required is a nip and tuck—an edit here, a minor character addition there, perhaps some slight refocus or a few updated references. Of course, in more extreme cases, substantial revision may be in order. Drastic cases might require a complete rewrite. But, rest assured, what-ever your need, we stand ready to serve, full confidentiality assured, of course."

"I'm not sure I really should be here," Joe Dixon said. He had been execu-tive vice president at Allied for nearly 12 years, the last several served under Sam Brown, who had turned the company around after hitting on a brilliant new marketing campaign. Dixon loved Sam as a person and as a boss. But Sam was getting ready to retire. He had announced it to the board two weeks ago. That's when Joe's life took a sudden downhill turn. He—and he believed Sam—had always assumed that he would take over whenever Sam decided to hang up his spurs. He knew Sam had recommended him as his successor, but apparently a couple of the board members favored an open search to fill the post. Translation: They wanted somebody younger and more exciting, some-body with a more exciting story.

"Of course, you should be here," Loki said. Dixon looked up. Loki now appeared to him to be taller, calmer, more in control. His voice took on a new tone, something between the stern voice of Mrs. Eastwick, his second grade teacher, and soft intonations his grandmother used to adopt when she was comforting him after a nightmare. "Is there something wrong?" Loki asked.

"No, it seems, well, I know this sounds crazy, but you seem to have changed," Dixon said, feeling like a complete fool.

"It's the lights," Loki reassured him. "They play tricks on the eyes."

Dixon nodded numbly. "Well, how do we get started?" he asked.

"Ah, yes, well indeed, getting started," Loki said. Dixon could have sworn Loki had changed again. Now he seemed more compact, yet softer. He reminded Dixon of a CFO at budget time—competent, tense, and equal parts servile and domineering. He really needed to get his eyes checked. Had it been a year already? "Are you all right, Mr. Dixon?" Loki asked.

"How did you know my name?" Dixon asked, suddenly nervous.

"Why, you introduced yourself when you came in," Loki said, his voice as smooth as the ice on the pond of Dixon's childhood memories. "Don't you remember? Poor man, you must be under a lot of pressure." Dixon didn't remember. But he was under a good deal of pressure. He needed this job.

"Look it's really quite simple," Loki said, steering Dixon toward a comfortable-looking sofa. "Just sit here, and we'll keep trying on stories until we find one that seems to fit.

"Let's see," Loki said, his appearance seeming to change once again. "We have the most comprehensive inventory of stories available. Ah, what do we have here? Earth Mother? Hardly appropriate. Earth Mover? I think not. Wizard? No, no, you don't strike me as the wizard type. Oh—here's my favorite—the Trickster, clearly the best of all the stories; but believe me, and this is the voice of considerable experience speaking, if this were the right story for you, you wouldn't need me. Besides, stories have to be appropriate at worst and authentic at best. So, let's see, ah here, we are the Caretaker; that ought to do nicely."

"Caretaker," said Dixon, "how's that going to make me look more exciting than some hot shot MBA from Wharton who just turned around a troubled midcap?"

"It isn't," yawned Loki. "That's the point. You don't want to look exciting; you want to look stable. Listen: Meet Joseph Dixon, whose steady and unassuming hand has helped steer Allied from a troubled company to one of the most solid players in the industry. Dixon provided the thread of continuity that kept the essential Allied engine churning as several CEOs tried their hand at the strategy du jour. It's Dixon who knows the soul of the company, who's committed his life and career to Allied, who's stayed with it in fair and foul. He's a known entity—strong, stable, reliable, self-effacing. For 12 years, he's been one heartbeat away from the top, always putting Allied's interests—and the interests of the board and shareholders—ahead of any personal political advantage. And, in this delicate time, it's Dixon who will require no ramp-up time, no on-boarding council, no transition period. He already sits on the top of the learning curve. And, given his temperament and track record, he can be counted on to be the perfect corporate steward, gently moving Allied ahead for years to come. He is, in short, the perfect choice to succeed Sam Brown, not just a worthy successor, but an inspired choice as the bridge from the present to the future."

"When you put it that way, it does seem to make sense," Dixon said.

"Of course, it makes sense," Loki snorted. During his monologue, he seemed to have taken on the persona of a televangelist. Beads of sweat had burst from his forehead, and his face seemed twisted with the pain of a sinner whose only wish is to be free of sin, if only for a moment.

"I'll take it," Dixon said. "Oh, and Mr. Loki, what kind of lights do you use? I want to make sure I never slip up and buy them."

"Oh, you mean how they make me appear to change my appearance," Loki said, his voice taking on all the innocence of a small child standing next to a broken vase. "Don't worry, Mr. Dixon, the lights wouldn't affect you the same way they affect me. I'd explain, but that's another story—and a very long story at that."

Chapter 11

APPLIED STORYTELLING 101: THE INDIVIDUAL

"Until lions have their historians, tales of the hunt shall always glorify the hunter."
—African proverb

"There is no agony like bearing an untold story inside of you."
—Maya Angelou

"When I look back on all these worries, I remember the story of the old man who said on his deathbed that he had had a lot of trouble in his life, most of which had never happened."
—Winston Churchill

"Strange as it may seem, my life is based on a true story."
—Ashleigh Brilliant

"People create stories create people; or rather stories create people create stories."
—Chinua Achebe

We really don't want to review all the storytelling principles already outlined in the previous chapters and apply them to how individuals can build and tell their own stories. After all, a story is a story is a story; and whether it's about a brand, a corporation, an industry, or an individual, the same principles apply. Stories often work on several levels simultaneously. Take the stories of George Washington admitting to chopping down the cherry tree or Abe Lincoln running miles to correct a change-making error. Both illustrate qualities of individual character and, at the same time, are parables on the value of honesty or the triumph of truth over self-interest. How you tell the story, where you place the emphasis in the story line, how you establish the context and characters, all determine which story the audience hears.

Let's take George Washington. We've already said the cherry tree story could be used to demonstrate individual character and, at the same time, the triumph of truth over self-interest. Told from his father's point of view, however, it could be a tale of good parenting and how to teach moral values. In this case, George himself is reduced to a bit player. It's the same story, with the same characters, describing the same events, but in the end, it's a much different story altogether. The story of virtue can, with a half-twist, become a lesson on vice. Imagine poor George, racked by guilt or tortured by the pain of carrying a lie inside him—a pressure so painful it can only be relieved through the purification of confession. Or, imagine George and his father estranged and reunited through a single act of defiance and redemption. You get the idea. The tools are always the same, but how you use them has everything to do with what you end up with.

The critical lesson here is that, given an even start, 10 good storytellers can tell 10 perfectly good (and possibly totally contradictory) tales. The Africans are right: Until the lions get a historian, the story of the hunt will always revolve around the hunters. What's true of lions, it seems, is also true of business or, in some cases, even the history of business.

Were Jay Gould, Andrew Carnegie, Leland Stanford, John D. Rockefeller, and J. Pierpont Morgan and their late-nineteenth-century and early-twentieth-century peers vital figures of American economic history, the embodiment of the American dream, the first modern capitalists? Or, were they as historian

Matthew Josephson suggested in his 1934 book, *The Robber Barons,* the lowest form of social and economic parasites, unfairly profiteering from illegal and secret deals and conspiracies against the working class?

It all depends, of course, on whom you ask. It's the nature of the personal mythos of the individual. Is Bill Gates a megalomaniacal monopolist or one of the greatest philanthropists alive? Is Steve Jobs a techno-also ran or the guy who's going to reinvent personal electronics? The final interpretation of whether a life is, or was, good or bad depends not so much on the facts, but on who can tell the most convincing (and often the most recent) story.

So, Why Tell the Story in the First Place?

We've done a fairly extensive job in the past few chapters discussing the "how" of business storytelling, so we thought we might take a little time to discuss the "why." Why should businesses worry about how to tell the story of an individual? There actually are several reasons, some solid and others, although just as compelling, of less value to the enterprise. Let's look at the most venial first—the ego of the founder or current leader.

Dismissing ego as irrelevant is a huge mistake. First, most leaders got where they are because they have a healthy ego. This ego will, directly or indirectly, lead somebody to tell the leader's story, to fuel the leader's myth. The process is all but unavoidable. The real question is who controls it.

Second, and equally important, is that people relate to people easier than they do to balance sheets. Discussing how certain modern leaders have become associated with the industries or innovations they lead, Paul Saffo, Roy Amara Fellow at the Institute for the Future, once noted the public's strong association between the leaders of a company, such as Bill Gates, and the technologies the company produces, such as operating systems. "Like all symbols, no small part of these associations are pure myth," he wrote. "For example, Bill Gates didn't invent the PC;

he didn't even write DOS, the predecessor to Windows. All this was done by others, and Bill is simply the poster boy for the personal computer revolution."[1]

Turning his attention to Larry Ellison, the founder of Oracle, Saffo notes, "Meanwhile, we wrap other myths atop our misunderstanding. Larry Ellison the person may be an arrogant jackass, but Ellison the icon is the embodiment of the hopes that drew Europeans to the new world a century ago. It is a myth embodied in his last name, itself the invention of the relative who reared him, chosen as an homage to the famous port of entry, Ellis Island."[2]

The process Saffo describes as "wrapping other myths on top of our misunderstanding" is known in academic myth-studying circles as bricolage, a term borrowed from the French word for a handyman (*bricoleur*) who uses broken pieces of older things to make wholly new things. Mythology expert Wendy Doniger believes that bricolage is an inherent element of all myth making and storytelling. "The very form of myth is a kind of self-imitation," she wrote, "the style of a myth immediately identifies its genre to its audience by mimicking the style of another myth. In substance, too, myths tell you what they have told you before and what you already know; they build a potentially infinite number of stories by rearranging a limited number of known mythic themes."[3]

Claude Lévi-Strauss, the father of structural anthropology, argued that there were any number of what he called mythemes, fragments of older stories that became the foundation of present and future stories—a sort of Chinese menu approach to storytelling in which the storyteller selects a character from Column A, a plot line from Column B, a moral from Column C, and so on.

In earlier chapters, we examined some of these mythemes. Now we want to look at some character archetypes from traditional mythology and storytelling to show how they can be applied to building the stories of an individual. This sampling, by the way, is just that. By no means does it represent anything approaching a full list of potential character models. That said, you might find one or two of these characters useful to experiment with:

- **The Earth Mother/Creator**

  A number of common elements lie at the heart of most Earth Mother stories: fertility, nurturing, origins, and wisdom. The Earth Mother character embodies all these along with overseeing the passage into birth or rebirth, and sometimes the cycle of birth to death. Earth Mother stories have found their way into every culture, including modern advertising. Chiffon Margarine made Mother Nature a cranky character displeased with butter substitutes. Not every business leader—assuming she's a woman—would want to aspire to Earth Mother status, but there's more than a touch of Earth Mother in Martha Stewart, which may explain why men and women so clearly not like her are attracted to her story anyway.

- **The Earth Mover**

  The stories of Prometheus, Atlas, and Paul Bunyan all draw on a character at once ultimately human in the most profound sense of the word and simultaneously superhuman. Modern corporate Earth Movers may not, like Atlas, carry the world on their backs, but they know how to send it spinning. Their stories are those of persons of power, who marshalling their strength bend the world to their will. Think Rudy Giuliani here or Jack Welch.

- **The General**

  Generals are great strategists and, when the need arises, great warriors. In ancient times, when stories of the General were first told, he (well usually, but not always, it was a he) rode out ahead of his troops, leading the charge against the enemy. Modern versions of the story find the General at the rear of the troops—directing, making thousands of instant decisions, and getting ready to sacrifice a few of the troops for the greater good. In business, the General (clearly no longer necessarily a man) is found busily reorganizing companies or leading merger and acquisition activity, although not always to a good or happy ending. Thanks to the archetype of the General, we get stories like those of Hewlett-Packard's Carly Fiorina and Henry R. Kravis, founder of leverage buyout house Kohlberg Kraviz Roberts & Co.

- **The Statesman**

  The Statesman's story is that of individuals who are politically savvy and have their focus firmly directed on the future, their feet planted on the ground, and their eyes turned to the stars. Statesmen are industry builders. Jack Valenti, the past chairman of the Academy of Motion Pictures Arts and Sciences, was a Statesman, as was Bill France, Jr., one of the founders of NASCAR.

- **The Alchemist/Wizard/Magician**

  One of our favorite characters, the Alchemist/Wizard/ Magician is an individual with the power to summon something from nothing or to create one thing out of something else, as in the transmutation of base metal into gold. This character is often portrayed as a hermit conjuror, a solitary mage who has the power to wrestle with the forces of nature alone, but who often is beholden to a power figure or society at large for support. Alan Kay, the father of portable computing, is a Wizard. So is George Lucas.

- **The Explorer/Discoverer**

  The Explorer plunges into the unknown just for the satisfaction of finding something nobody else has ever seen. The search itself is always the greatest part of the Explorer's reward. Thomas Edison and George Washington Carver were Explorers. Amazon.com's Jeff Bezos is also an

Explorer, one who ventured into cyberspace and found a viable commercial niche no one else was seriously even thinking about.

- **The Trickster/Jester**

  If we've got an absolute favorite on this list, this may be it. The story of the Trickster is the story of the changeling, the agent provocateur, the chameleon, who appears to be one thing but is really quite another. The Jester, of course, is the deadly serious clown, the only figure allowed to tell the king the truth or openly mock the court. Sadly, the corporate world doesn't tolerate Jesters too well. On the other hand, the corporate tendency to seek out and kill internal staff Jesters has created a whole new industry—modern business consulting. It is, after all, the consultant who has the right to tell the CEO the truth that everybody in the company already knows but is either afraid or unable to communicate. James O. McKinsey and Tom Kearney might be considered the patron saints of Tricksters/Jesters.

- **The Faithful Servant/Caretaker**

  The story of the Caretaker has a surprising amount of power. IBM's Tom Watson, Jr., was a great leader in his own right, but he was cast in the mold of a steward for the business his father had built. Lee Iacocca came to Chrysler as a Caretaker leader for the business. His mission: to help the company survive until the next watch. The classic model for this story is, of course, the pope, whose stated mission is to act as the shepherd of the flock until the big boss gets back.

- **The Judge/Wise Man**

  Few people in the business world fit easily into the role of the Judge or Wise Man, but we think Warren Buffet and Peter Drucker come pretty close: Buffet, for his calm weighing of facts and uncanny ability to see core values in companies, and the late Dr. Drucker for his ability to cut through the limitations and distractions of the present and capture the practical essence of the future.

- **The Artisan**

  The story of the Artisan is always closely associated with the art. Leo Fender, one of the fathers of the modern electric guitar, is a great example of an Artisan, as was the late Jim Henson, the "father" of the Muppets.

We could go on and on, but we trust you get the idea. If you want to find out what story to tell, the best place to start is to read the stories of individuals you like or would like to be compared to. Here are just a few cautionary rules for the road:

1. Remember, characters in a story don't have to be "real" to be "real," as we discovered in 2006, when a more metro-sexual Ken returned to court Barbie, who it turns out, has her own real-world press agent. Tony the Tiger, Betty Crocker, the Keebler elves, the Pillsbury Doughboy, and even Uncle Ben and Aunt Jemima have all effectively pitched food products. The point is that if you build a credible enough story, the story's characters can take on all the properties of actual individuals in the audience's mind. This has never been truer than it is today. Celebrity "news" often pre-empts reporting of significant economic, political, or social news. Britney Spears shaving her hair—it was just a haircut after all—was apparently seen by many news sources as more critical than Scooter Libby's obstruction of justice trial. The same was true for the rather ghoulish details of the Anna Nicole Smith and James Brown burial controversies.

2. If you're building an individual story, always keep in mind that there are two basic paths you can follow. An individual can be portrayed as having always embodied certain

characteristics. Abe Lincoln was honest even as a teenager, for example. Or, he or she can develop certain characteristics as the result of a revelation or deeply impactful experience or test of character, as was the case when Saul of Tarsus was knocked off his horse by God and blinded. Which you choose to tell is probably less important than thinking about which version to use. Politicians in particular always seem to get this one wrong. They often portray themselves as having always had certain qualities—"As a district attorney, Candidate X was always tough on crime"; "Her humble beginnings in the rural heartland imbued Candidate Y with a rich sense of the power of family and community and taught her the value of hard work"—only to have to go back and explain why their position on certain critical, high-profile issues has changed in light of some sort of conversion experience.

3. Building up an individual's story is often useful in the business world. The danger is that sometimes characters can outgrow a company and become larger than life. When this happens in business, the person gains too much leverage in the company, a situation that always leads to temporary disaster until it's resolved. There's a reason Steve Jobs had to leave Apple the first time. Sometimes the characters are only gargantuan in their own minds. I'm sure we've all known people who boasted that a company would never survive without them. Invariably, they were wrong.

4. Once again, when telling stories, consistency is critical. Audiences suspend credibility in the case of fairy tales, myths, and movies, but they're much less forgiving when it comes to real life. It's all right when your story takes you from one role to another provided you're moving along a linear path, as in the case of George W. Bush, who moved from Ivy League party animal to a homespun Texas born-again Christian. But if George spends his time after he

retires from office chasing Hooters waitresses, whatever is left of the public bloom will fade off his rose. This might be what saved Bill Clinton. After Jennifer Flowers, et al., Monica Lewinsky fit into the story we had already woven around the president.

5. Characters can only make sense in context. Don't try to tell your story—or the story of any individual—outside of a context that supports it. Remember, we're practicing bricolage here, so our recombining of pieces into a new mosaic can't exceed the frame size.

6. Credibility is critical. You can fool all of the people some of the time and some of the people all of the time, but you shouldn't. If your story isn't credible, any number of forces from the media, to regulators, to your shareholders (if you're the CEO), or your boss (if you're in middle management) will try to poke holes in it.

7. Great stories are unambiguous, and the moral of your story should be clear as a bell. After all, what's the point of telling a story if nobody gets the point?

8. Finally, never ever fall in love with your own story. Remember the moral of the story of Narcissus, one of the most beautiful men to walk the earth. The gods told his parents he would have a long life, provided he never saw his own image. One day Narcissus happened along a pond. Gazing into the pond, he saw his reflection for the first time. Transfixed, he grew closer and closer to the image until he finally drowned trying to touch it. It's a story Al Dunlop should have read before he went to Sunbeam and one somebody should read to Paris Hilton.

One last note: Remember that the rules of bricolage suggest that today's story will one day be broken up and reassembled into another story. It can happen in an instant. We leave you with this quote from Larry Weber's *The Provocateur,* a study of the best-of-breed new leaders, circa 2001:

> Leaders who come to mind when you think of an industry have achieved brand status. If you think of an industry, the name that comes immediately to mind is the brand. Think of the energy industry–Jeffrey Skilling at Enron. He took a commodity and achieved a brand. By also building himself as a brand (even if inadvertently and unconsciously) and having a separate brand with Enron, Skilling has built a successful community.[4]

As Billie Holiday once sang, "What a difference a day makes."

"*Good afternoon Mr. Loki*. It's so good to see you again," Mary Strong said, ushering Aldous Loki toward a seat in the small but tastefully appointed private conference room adjacent to her office.

"Oh, no, Ms. Strong, the pleasure is most certainly all mine," said Loki, whose chiseled good looks now reminded Strong a bit of Gregory Peck, although she had certainly gotten a much more Val Kilmerish vibe the first time they met.

"Anything wrong?" Loki asked solicitously.

"It's nothing really," Strong stammered. "It's just that for some silly reason I seemed to remember you looking a bit different, that's all."

"Well, don't worry," Loki reassured her. "People often tell me that I remind them of somebody else—a variety of other people, as it turns out. I just have that kind of face. Besides, I'm certain you've had lots of candidates through this room in the past few weeks. It's easy to get us mixed up after a while. Or, maybe it's just the lights."

"Well," Strong said, trying to regain control of the interview, "I spoke to Joe Dixon over at Allied, and he couldn't have recommended you in any stronger terms. I don't know what you did for him, but you clearly made a big impression on him."

"I'm sure Joe was just being kind," Loki said, now looking for all the world like Strong's father when he contentedly leaned back from the Sunday dinner table. "It was really nothing."

"No, on the contrary, I'm sure you're just being modest, Mr. Loki," Strong blurted, surprised how fast the words seemed to fly out of her mouth. Trying to get a grip on herself, she turned to the open file before her. "Your credentials are very impressive," she said. "Let's see, you were head of public relations for Valhalla Enterprises in Oslo, COO of Coyote Productions in Sante Fe, president of Hermes Holdings in Athens, and, of course, CEO of Custom Tales here. Why, I see you even worked with the Yoruba tribe in Nigeria on something called Project Eshu. Did I pronounce that correctly? That must have been fascinating. Frankly, with credentials like this, I'm not sure why you want to come to work for us."

Loki, who suddenly to Strong seemed the soul of world weariness, stood up and walked almost painfully to the window. "May I be frank, Ms. Strong?" he asked, a supplicant begging absolution for the most minor of sins. "It's true I've traveled the world and held, what I'm sure from the outside, appear to be a host of fascinating positions. And it's true that my own firm, Custom Tales, does scratch that entrepreneurial itch I'm sure we all feel from time to time. But the burdens are endless. I'm anxious to get back in the harness, work with a team, be part of something bigger them myself. I miss the camaraderie of like-minded souls chasing a common goal. Think of me as more like Michael Jordan or Babe Ruth and less like Lance Armstrong or Tiger Woods. I'm sure you understand."

In fact, Mary Strong did not understand. She hated people who used sports analogies. If she didn't work for Joe Dixon's brother-in-law, she wouldn't have been interviewing candidates for a corporate storyteller position. Instead, like every other VP of HR, she would have been evaluating the latest crop of bright young things who, each year, having found their collective way out of the nation's top five B-schools, stormed the gates of American commerce looking to start in what they all insisted on referring to as "a CxO slot."

"I have to confess, Mr. Loki, I'm rather new at all this storytelling business," said Strong.

"Aren't we all," cooed Loki, who, in the filtered sunlight pouring through the window, looked and even sounded a bit like Bing Crosby during his *Bells of St. Mary's* and *Going My Way* period. "The truth is, it's all rather simple. You see, there are story finders whose gift it is to select just the right story to fit the current need from a brand launch to repositioning the CEO—a bit of what I do at Custom Tales. Then there is the storyteller, the person who actually frames the story—tailoring it here and there, smoothing it over, making it entertaining—you get the picture. You sometimes find them working in advertising agencies. Then there are the story sellers, those gifted by the gods with the ability to communicate the perfect story to any audience. Think of your marketing people here. Finally, there are the story storers, the keepers of the company's mythology, if you will. They are the guardians of a business or brand's fairy tales, the historians of the corporate message over time."

"I see," said Strong, surprised at the echo of breathlessness in her own voice. "And, please don't take this the wrong way, Mr. Loki, but we in HR recognize that a human being is an amalgam of strengths and weaknesses. So...with that in mind...which of these areas do you feel you are you good at and where, in your own estimation, of course, are you weakest?"

Loki smiled, and Strong felt herself slipping away like the time Fred Reiss had almost hypnotized her in college. "Oh, yes, Ms. Strong, it's quite true that humans are a mishmash of strengths and weaknesses. But I thought we were talking about me," Loki said as he suddenly grew larger and luminescent. "I'm good at all four things. Wouldn't you agree?"

"Oh, yes," Strong said, her now husky voice more mechanical than human, as though a set of skilled fingers were playing her vocal chords like an instrument. "Tell me, Mr. Loki, would you consider accepting the position?"

"Why, of course, Ms. Strong," Loki said. "I thought you'd never ask."

Chapter 12

THE STORYTELLER'S TOOLBOX

"From religion to philosophy, from alchemy to chemistry, from legend to history, the social organization of knowledge changes as a new elite comes in to challenge the old authorities. But this movement is not simply a linear and one-directional shift toward increasing rationalization and demystification; when the rational historian has come in to take away authority from the mystical and tribal bard, the artist has returned to create new forms of expression to resacrilize, re-enchant, remythologize."

—William Irwin Thompson

"Telling the proper stories is as if you were approaching the throne of heaven in a fiery chariot."

—Baal Shem Tov

"There have been great societies that did not use the wheel, but there have been no societies that did not tell stories."

—Ursula K. LeGuin

"The greatest stories are those that resonate our beginnings and intuit our endings, our mysterious origins and our numinous destinies, and dissolve them both into one."

—Ben Okri

"Every story you tell is your own story."

—Joseph Campbell

Storytelling's core elements are timeless. As we've discussed in earlier chapters, there is a standard list of characters to choose from and a standard list of plots for those characters to act out. But in storytelling, context and time and method of delivery can become even more important than the story itself.

Back to Basics

Before we go much further, let's revisit why we are worried about storytelling in the first place. Stories reach us on several levels simultaneously. We can thrill to an adventure or emotionally identify with a character and still use reason and logic to derive a fairly concrete message that we can then apply to other contexts. Understanding what stories resonate with a target audience also begins to tell us a great deal about that audience. Storytelling is also an amazingly effective method of knowledge transfer and a powerful tool for message retention. Since the beginning of human society, people have used stories to explain away, or cultivate, mystery. Great stories, as noted earlier, allow an audience member to become personally involved and emotionally integrated into your story.

Stories also have the ability to raise the venial and banal to the level of extraordinary and entertaining. The day-to-day struggles to establish a company or be competitive in a market aren't nearly as exciting as stories about that struggle. Saying that Joe Miller, owner of Miller's Hardware, lowered the price of screwdrivers by 16 percent, rechargeable drills by 23 percent, light bulbs by 50 percent, and wood screws by 7 percent is simply not as interesting as a story that begins like this:

> Faced with the reality of a Wal-Mart entry into his town, a community he and his family had served for four generations and more than 90 years, Joe Miller decided to face Wal-Mart head on. If some out-of-town chain thought it could buy the loyalty of the citizens of Anytown with some

cheap prices on power drills, Miller would show them they were wrong. Of course, Joe was a realist. He knew his neighbors and knew there was only so far working-class people could go, even if it meant turning their back on a family they had known all their lives, who had extended them credit when the plant closed, and who sponsored their kid's softball team the same way it had sponsored theirs and their parent's. So Joe lowered his prices—not across the board, but on those items he knew his customers prized the most. He knew he was facing a battle for survival, and so he prepared himself to go to war. He kept a smile on his face in front of Sue and the kids, but privately Joe was scared to death. Wal-Mart had buried a lot of companies like his, and Joe knew that come April 3 when the store opened, he was in for the fight of his life—and maybe quite literally a fight for his life.

What the best storytelling does is establish a three-way connection among the audience, the storyteller, and the characters in the story. After that connection has been established, it can facilitate any number of ends. A logical starting point is to engage the audience in a dialogue with your company. This can be accomplished either through the creation of an ongoing story line or by giving them a memorable character to relate to. Mr. Whipple, the character who embodies Charmin, fighting his endless battle to end squeezing—only to succumb to the squeezing urge himself—is a much warmer story than "We're Procter & Gamble, and we make bathroom tissue."

If Travelocity chose to tell its story this way, "Hey, we can get you a cheap hotel room in Omaha," we doubt that we'd think about the company much differently than we do Orbitz or your local discount travel agent. Add a story of a peripatetic lawn gnome to the equation, and suddenly the story becomes far more engaging. Through a series of television ads and now his own website, the gnome puts a silly resin face on an otherwise plain vanilla service offering. Or, as the company explains:

Ever since our gnome friend was...er...gnomenapped from his owner's front yard in North Carolina, he's been jetting all over the world with his captors. Thanks to the ease of Travelocity, he's been schussing down snowy slopes, sailing and snorkeling in the Caribbean, cashing in at the black-jack tables in Vegas, taking spontaneous road trips—and loving every minute of it! While the practice of gnome-nabbing has been going on for years, this particular gnome has achieved a sort of celebrity-status, appearing on television and radio ads, posing for photo shoots in exotic locales, and getting recognized in airports across the country. He's even earned a prestigious title: The Roaming Gnome.[1]

Sometimes the story grows to become a product line in-and-of-itself. In Travelocity's case, true gnome aficionados can purchase their very own full-size gnome statue ($64.95), a small gnome statue ($19.99), or a gnome stress reliever ($4.95). Also available are the usual T-shirts, umbrellas, beach towels, travel mugs, and the somewhat more unusual gnome "dress up magnet."

Almost all corporate stories tell you what the company is about, but they can achieve this end through a variety of means. They can tell a story about the company, its origins, and its growth. They can also tell the story of the founder, the current top executive or, as in the case of Travelocity, even the company's icon.

Smart companies often opt to tell stories about customers—not testimonials per se, but rather stories illustrating some basic character or quality of a company or its products. Finally, you can tell the story of products themselves. Some people even believe that storytelling itself will become a product.

In *The Dream Society*, Rolf Jensen wrote about a future in which "We will purchase 'storytelling' of all sorts in our spare time: stories about leisure time where the family may reinforce its sense of togetherness, after workdays where not enough time has been spent with one another. This might be an inspiring story told through a theme restaurant, or it might be the great story from the South Pole. It could also be the rock concert or the sports event where feelings are not only allowed, they are the whole point."[2]

Some corporate storytellers like to discuss a subset of corporate stories they call "in-house company stories." These stories, intended for internal audiences, help build a common culture, establish organizational identity, convey shared values named goals, and celebrate individual or group achievements. As Christopher Locke has noted, "Today we need anthems more than analysis. We need to tell new and deeper, larger stories. Stories about ourselves—the kind of creatures who invent them, and why their creation is so important. Stories about why we can't afford to lose such a precious human legacy in a din of charlatanism and slobbering artless venality."[3]

Locke was one of the coauthors of *The Cluetrain Manifesto: The End of Business as Usual,* which begins with 95 theses, several addressing the sterility of the traditional corporate voice.[4] Our vote goes to companies that understand that in the Post-Information Age—or whatever you want to call the current evolving commercial environment—communication is less linear and more like a Möbius strip or loop. For the uninitiated, a Möbius strip is what scientists refer to as "a nonorientable surface." If you want to make one, just take a strip of paper, twist the strip once and glue the ends together. You should end up with a strip that has no top or bottom surface in the conventional sense. You can draw a line on the strip and move from front to back without ever having to raise your pen or pencil off the paper.

The Möbius strip provides us with what we feel is one of the most effective metaphors for corporate storytelling. Forget what the experts tell you—there is no inside- or outside-the-corporation communication anymore. It's easy to date the fall of the Great Corporate Wall to the beginning of the Internet, but it's not entirely accurate. Clearly, the Internet allows messages to pass more easily inside and outside companies, but other factors from industry consolidation; to a general reduction of employee loyalty to the corporation (and vice versa); and a growing abhorrence for the idea of staying at one job for one's entire business life all helped facilitate the decline of "inside-only" communications.

This doesn't mean you can't have messaging whose primary target is inside or outside the company walls. It does mean you'd be well advised not to believe that the messaging stops at its intended target. Look at how much trouble the Bush administration has had with controlling messages concerning national security in an environment where the punishments for breaching a confidence can be—to say the least—severe, and you begin to get some idea of exactly how tough it is to keep internal stories inside the company.

What it does mean is that your "inside target" stories have to have the same content quality as those intended for "outside" audiences. Their language has to be engaging. Their plots have to exciting. Above all, the characters have to be credible and not some one-dimensional, self-serving cardboard cut-out versions of a real character.

Finally, it's really important to remember that although storytelling is a perennial activity, stories themselves have definite life cycles. Greek mythology, which most of us are familiar with even if it's just through television and the movies, provides an effective case study of how the nature and impact of a story can change over time.

The Death of Zeus, Inc.: A Case Study in How to Lose a Cosmic Monopoly

It's a long fall from being a hero on top of Mt. Olympus to being Angelina Jolie's diaper bag carrier, but that's the cruel fate suffered by Achilles and shared, in one form or another, by the rest of the Greek gods, demigods, and heroes. One minute Achilles was being lionized for eternity in marble and epic poetry so that no one would ever forget his name. A scant few centuries later, he was reduced to being portrayed by a sulking Brad Pitt in the highly forgettable movie *Troy*. For the ancient Greeks, the stories of Zeus, Hera, Aphrodite, and Athena and their relatives and mortal lovers explained everything from the structure of the physical universe to why one warring side or another was victorious. In a few short centuries, however, the gods' stories moved from sacred truth to popular myth. And there's a lesson here for every company content to rest on past versions of their story.

Describing ancient Greece from the Minoan period (circa 1400 B.C.E.) until the end of Greece's dark ages (about 800 B.C.E.), Kenneth C. Davis wrote, "Myth played a central role in Greek life and society; they were at the core of religious observances and entertainment. Along with language and a common culture, myths provided a bond that no central Greek government ever could."[5] Remember what we now know as the Greek myths were once the integral fabric and universal truths that held together what was once the most developed of all Western civilizations.

Within the context of ancient Greece, the stories of the gods were nothing more or less than the retelling of unquestioned truths (truths, by the way, that helped explain everything from history to volcanic eruption). But somewhere around the eighth century B.C.E., a new kind of storyteller emerged in Greece. His name was Homer, the author of the *Iliad* and the *Odyssey*. In Homer's version of the Greek past, the gods became much more human. What had, for centuries, been theology became, in Homer's telling, a cosmic soap opera with gods and goddesses punishing each other for illicit affairs and playing with human lives as pawns. In short, the stuff of popular entertainment.

The deathblow to the sacredness of the Greek god tales began around 595 B.C.E. Its epicenter was the seaport city of Miletus on the western shore of Ionia (the birthplace of Homer) in Asia Minor, a hop, skip, and jump across the Aegean Sea from Athens. Miletus was also the birthplace of Western philosophy. The thinkers it produced have come to be known as the Milesians, Ionians, or sometimes just the Pre-Socratics.[6] The Pre-Socratics pursued thoughtful answers to questions previously answered by blind belief. They were simultaneously both the earliest philosophers and the earliest scientists. They were also, as it turned out, at the very least, principal accessories in the death of the Greek gods.

The real god killers, of course, were Socrates (470 B.C.E.), his student Plato (428 or 427 B.C.E.), and Plato's student Aristotle (384 B.C.E.). These three thinkers undermined the Greek's primitive faith-based model of the universe, replacing it with a more rigorous model based on the strict application of tools, ranging from logic and formal theories or rhetoric; to consistent ethical and political models; to scientific observation and categorization. These early philosopher-scientists didn't necessarily set out to destroy the gods. It was just that in the new intellectual context they created, there wasn't much room left for a divine pantheon made up of a gaggle of squabbling gods and demigods. The fall of the Greek gods illustrates an interesting quality of myth. The rise of modernism created a dynamic tension between belief systems and faith systems—in this case, between religion and science. All myths—and most stories—draw their energy from that tension.

The new story of a rational, knowable, predictable, and therefore ultimately controllable universe became more relevant than the ancient tales of the lusty, brutish, capricious, and vain gods who changed the fate of lives and nations on a whim or as a petty act of vengeance. The fact that we still remember the Greek gods at all—even as plot fillers for bad movies such as *Troy*, television series such as *Hercules* and *Xena: Warrior Princess*, and cartoons—speaks volumes about the power of the stories that surround them. They also show us the danger in pushing stories that are no longer relevant, or at the very least have lost their ability to engage audiences because of a radical change of context. Remember, all stories have to remain relevant to the times they are told in to be effective. So, what dynamics are necessary for a story to be effective?

Tell Me Why (and Who and How and What It All Means)

Constructing a corporate story is, in many respects, not that much different from sitting around a campfire exchanging tales. It just should have a different aim. All the campfire storytellers have to do is capture the imagination of their audience. They're free to use any number of plot devices, from horror to humor and mystery to romance. Not all of these storytelling gambits are appropriate to all corporate messaging. So, how do you go about building the story of your business?

There are probably any number of storytellers out there who would advise you to start with a character. We suppose that's fine if your intention is to build the image of an individual, but we think (short of aggrandizing a CEO or founder) it's probably best to start with a principle, a value, or a moral. In other words, before you build your story, carefully consider what you want the audience to take away from it.

It's also important to remember what stories are not.

They are not unadorned assertions of fact. "Miracle Soap gets your clothes 90 times cleaner than other laundry liquids" isn't a story. It's a product claim. It lacks theme, plot development, and characters. The best stories tend to be affirmations rather than negations. Countering an unfavorable media article or broadcast with your version of the facts is not a story—it's spin. There's no context or meaning outside your self-interest. Stories are complete in-and-of themselves. They take a character or set of characters from point A to point B and leave you with a conclusion—something to consider or a new point of view. Try as most marketers might—with few exceptions—they don't produce real stories.

So, let's assume that you've settled on a principle and you've successfully wrapped it around a character. You want him or her or it (in the case of a company) to be sympathetic. Don't oversell! Remember that one of the keys to great storytelling is the ability to convey complex, and often abstract, ideas in simple language. Make the character complete and interesting, but not so complicated you begin to build in an unwanted sense of ambiguity that can—and in most cases will—obscure your message.

Next, put that character in a context that both draws the audience's attention and sets a credible stage for the rest of the story. Get the context wrong, and the story just won't make any sense. Get it right, and the story will almost begin to tell itself.

After you've settled on a moral, main character, and context, you need to select a plot for theme. Again, we recommend using any of the standard plots we've outlined in earlier chapters. Why a standard plot? Well, it's pretty hard to get away from them, and selecting a well-known plot—or theme—makes it easier for the audience to identify with your story.

Now it's time to begin telling your story. We'd suggest you try to tell "the" story of your company, brand, product, service, or relationship with customers. Those stories about real families saving money or being rescued by Allstate Insurance agents work, but only because Allstate has spent years telling audiences "the" story of how they are the "good hands" people. The current crop of Allstate stories reinforces "the" Allstate story. They don't define the company; they reinforce what, one hopes, the audience already believes in the same way that one of the Greek myths of Zeus' philandering around with mortals illustrated his character but didn't define his divinity.

Next it's time to "storyboard" or outline your story.

You know who you're starting with, and you know where you're going, but what happens in the middle? Your story should be direct, fast paced, and get you to the message. The stories of Henry Ford paying workers $5 a day, saying that you could buy any color Model T you wanted as long as it was black, and building one of the first large industrial assembly lines are all great stories reinforcing Ford's character as a shrewd pragmatist who understood the basic elements of industrial success. Reading how he decided on a T-2577 NOS U-Joint in the 1909–1927 Model Ts or how the brake cam specs were changed in 1926 is great information for an automotive restorer, but it doesn't do much for the story of how a simple man rose to become one of America's great industrialists.

It's critical to remember that you're crafting a story for an audience, not for yourself. What you think is important might not in fact mean much to a disinterested third party. The dynamics of most story construction are fairly simple. You establish your characters and an initial context; something changes, motivating an action on these characters' parts; the story reaches a turning point or crisis where some quality or qualities of the main character are tapped to address the crisis; the crisis is resolved or the turning point is passed; and the story moves toward resolution and message.

Sitting Around the Digital Campfire

The twenty-first century may be remembered as storytelling's greatest era. Never before has it been possible to disseminate a story—true, false, real, or imaginary—so quickly and so completely. With a simple keystroke, your story—or a story about you—can fly through cyberspace to anyone with the potential for connectivity. Through blogging and other interactive activities, the Internet has opened up a new era of serial storytelling, one in which I start the story and you—or a hundred "you"s—finish it for me. MySpace, Facebook, Flickr, YouTube, and similar websites allow millions of young people to share their versions of their stories with audiences from their next-door neighbor to someone living 3,000 miles away. Often, stories communicate whom they would like to be more than who they really are. But the Internet isn't the only thing facilitating storytelling.

CNN and other cable news networks have a round-the-clock need for content, food for the 24/7 cable media beast. Every cable channel and the major networks are desperate for content, let alone "unique" content. So is 24-hour talk radio. As we add communication connectivity and broadcast and narrowcast capacity, we exponentially increase our need for content. The market for stories is definitely a bull market. Of course, just because we can tell our stories across a variety of forums doesn't necessarily mean we should.

We believe selecting the method for delivering stories will become at least as critical to storytelling success as selecting the right context for the story itself.

Certain stories are more appropriate for certain communications vehicles and venues. If your story is aimed at building community for a certain class of biker, a blog might be effective, and perhaps a narrowcast physical venue such as a Harley-Davidson dealer or bike rally. On the other hand, if you're trying to tell a corporate growth story, a website, an analysts' meeting, and collateral sales materials may all be viable channels. Remember, the endgame here is engagement—building a meaningful and sustainable relationship with an audience, one audience member at a time.

Take a Cue from Social Science

We're both proponents of applying the social sciences to business. For us, there really aren't business problems—just problems associated with business cultures. So, we suggest that you add a little social science learning to your storytelling toolbox.

Archaeology, for example, can tell us a good deal about the effective creation and use of artifacts. Many of the artifacts of modern commerce—the clamshell fast-food box, disposable items from lighters to cameras, high-technology items that are inherently obsolete as opposed to the products of the old industrial technology era that had built-in obsolescence, reams of office paper waiting to be shredded, and the shredder itself—are symbols of a culture in which artifacts are fragile, perishable, and transitory. Ask yourself, what does your company make or do that will survive much past the short term? Now think of the story of Alexander the Great, who had oversized armor and weapons buried all over Asia Minor, so that, centuries after he was dead, men would marvel at how an army of apparent giants had conquered their world.

Anthropology has a great deal to teach us about effective symbology and iconography. There's a reason why consumers will tattoo some logos on their arms and faces, and why they cut other logos off products or won't be caught dead wearing them at all. Symbols are powerful and, effectively used, can go a long way toward telling or reinforcing your story.

Psychology has shadowed myth making almost from its inception. Myths became the primary research materials of psychology's earliest pioneers such as Carl Jung and Sigmund Freud. "Myth," Jung wrote, "says a Church Father, is 'what is believed always, everywhere, by everybody'; hence the man who thinks he can live without myth, or outside it, is an exception. He is like one uprooted, having no true link either with the past, or with the ancestral life which continues within him, or yet with contemporary human society. He does not live in a house like other men, but lives a life of his own sunk in a subjective mania of his devising, which he believes to be the newly discovered truth."[7] As Jung might have noted, a myth is a public dream, and a dream is a private myth.

Political science and social psychology both provide excellent— if often alarming—examples of the power and use of storytelling. Adolf Hitler was a master storyteller. In fact, Hitler encouraged Alfred Rosenberg, one of the principal ideologists of the Nazi Party and editor of the Nazi paper *Völkischer Beobachter*, to write *The Myth of the Twentieth Century* (*Der Mythus des zwanzigsten Jahrhunderts*), sort of a back story in support of the story of Aryan supremacy. It's a book, by the way, according to all the historical evidence, that the German dictator never bothered to read himself.

Whether Hitler read it or not, Rosenberg's book was the second most popular book on the Nazi Party reading list. There's a little something in it for every armchair fascist. It tells the story of migrating hordes from Atlantis who established Nordic culture and with it the Aryan master race. According to Rosenberg, the Aryans advanced across the earth in four successive waves: first to North Africa (an Indo-Aryan migration to Persia and India), then the Doric Greeks, Latins, and the Teutonic colonization by Germanic Western Europe. Although he was a professed Christian, Rosenberg's book is full of Teutonic gods and nature worship. The bottom line of myth is that the Germans are God's chosen people and Hitler was the new Messiah, sent by God to help them fulfill their destiny. The logic was silly, strained, or nonexistent. The history is absurd and convoluted. Nevertheless, despite its obvious flaws and foolishness, the story is one that, unfortunately, a large number of people were more than prepared to accept as gospel.

Our point here is that storytelling and myth making aren't just the stuff of poets and novelists. They can, in fact, be viable subjects for analysis and formal study by respected social scientists — a point all those who think of these activities as unbusinesslike would be well served to remember.

Four Variations on a Theme

We want to close this toolbox chapter with four positions or roles you can take in relation to stories. The first is the role of the Story Finder. Before you can tell a story, you need to find one, preferably an authentic one, and, even more important, one you can legitimately claim as your own. We're all walking collections of stories—stories we learned at home, at school, from our friends and coworkers, in church, from old books, and from pop culture. Finding the right story is critical and not always as easy as it seems. Finding the right personal story is an exercise in self-knowledge and analysis. The same is true on a slightly broader scale with finding the right corporate story.

After the right story has been "found," somebody needs to communicate it, and communication is the job of the Storyteller and the Story Seller. As we hope you see by now, telling a story is an art form. It's an art form we believe most people can master. But mastering it requires serious effort. Selling a story may, in many ways, be easier than telling one. You just have to make sure you're selling the right story to the right audience at the right time through the right venue. Connectivity and engagement are the keys to successful storytelling and selling, and they depend on a deep and profound understanding of who the customers are and where their emotional triggers can be found.

Finally, there are Story Storers, generally companies, whose job it is to aggressively archive and repackage their organization's stories. The widespread popularity of *The Da Vinci Code* and the dozens of similar books it spawned in its wake indicates a predisposition on the part of the reading public to believe that the Vatican is the ultimate Story Storer. There's perhaps a certain ironic symmetry to the fact that a story about story storing is one of the most popular stories being told and sold today.

The bottom line is that there's an awful lot to this business of storytelling. It shouldn't be approached in a haphazard manner. The good news is that most of the heavy lifting surrounding storytelling has already been done. All you really need to make storytelling a vital element of your corporate toolbox is a willingness to begin. Some, like Rolf Jensen, whom we quoted earlier in this chapter, believe that stories will be the ultimate products in this century. "The physical products representing the stories may be produced anywhere in the world, but this is not where the biggest profits lie," Jensen wrote. "The money is made through selling the stories themselves."[8]

In a world where so many "truths" are transitory, where products are designed to be disposable, where corporate integrity is dissected every night on CNN, where consumers have grown so skeptical that they'd rather believe nothing than run the risk of appearing to be fools, and where heroes and villains are often the same person just on a different day, myths and stories provide sources of constant values over time. That's why we go back to them, over and over again. Companies that master the art of storytelling enjoy a sustainable advantage over their competition because, in uncertain times, we all want a good story to reassure us.

Rolf Jensen suggests that, in this century, stories will surpass pure products as a source of revenue. We don't know whether he is right, but we are confident that the market for stories has never been better and that the future of business belongs to effective corporate storytellers.

What exactly will that future look like? Well, that's another story for another time.

Epilogue

A NEW STORY FOR A NEW CENTURY

"The truth is more important than the facts."
—Frank Lloyd Wright

"We are here to hand one another on."
—Walker Percy

"Set forth thy tale, and tarry not the time."
—Geoffrey Chaucer

We couldn't really end this book without trying just one more little experiment in storytelling. We were interested in seeing whether, in fact, a new myth could be written for the twenty-first century, one centering on something we believe will be critical to all of us by the end of this century, if not much, much sooner. Of course, a really new kind of story would require a unique character, one that traditional storytellers couldn't even imagine. We offer this tale of such a character with all due apologies to Jim Morrison's Mr. Mojo Risin'. By the way, that's a big hint for all you cryptography fans out there. We call this final story...

The Saga of Primus Loch

Primus Loch gained consciousness on April 3, 2027, at precisely 3:37 a.m. He remembered by turns who he was, the exact time and date, and frighteningly, that he had absolutely no clue as to where he was or what he was doing there. Struggling to move, Primus found himself oddly confined. Although he couldn't feel anything tying him down, he was incapable of any kind of motion. "I'm drugged," he thought. "That's it—I'm drugged and paralyzed." Drugs might explain his inability to move, but they failed to explain his almost crystal clear mental state. It was, he thought, a clarity unlike anything he could ever recall.

His perceptions—or more correctly, his perceptions of everything but himself—were equally vivid. He sensed colors so vibrant he felt he should be able to touch them. He was momentarily deafened as a hundred sounds flooded his ears at once. Bizarrely, he was somehow able to categorize each sound almost as soon as he heard it. Primus's brain quickly sorted what had begun as a cacophonous wall of sound into a neatly arranged aural inventory. Somehow Primus knew he was in a room and that he was surrounded by people making every effort not to make a sound. He was aware of the whir of microprocessors, the steady waves of central air-driven breezes bouncing off a series of objects of different heights and densities. Amazingly, he somehow knew that mold was starting to grow next to a very slight leak in a drain. The mold was all but invisible. Its existence was protected against attacks by the cleaning crew, who, Primus realized, concentrated their efforts primarily on the areas of the room that could be easily seen, glossing over any surface that lay behind a door or drawer.

He began to feel the panic rise in his brain. He fought back the urge to scream. Now wasn't the time to start losing it. Time to be cool. Time to assess and then take the appropriate action. What was he doing here? And where, for that matter, was here? Primus seemed trapped in something inside the room, undetected by the others who were clearly going about the day oblivious to the fact that he either existed or needed their help to escape.

To tell the truth, Primus really didn't feel exactly trapped. He just wasn't free to go. He really didn't feel like he was being held captive at all. In fact, he almost felt that he belonged here, again, wherever *here* was. Primus culled through his memory again. He seemed to have perfect recall of almost everything—everything that is, except who he really was and what he was doing in this strange, but now somehow comforting, room.

"Maybe I'm in a coma," he thought. "Maybe when you're in a coma it looks to your doctors and nurses and visitors like nothing is registering, but the truth is your brain is still going. Maybe your brain never turns off." The fear that he had been choking back suddenly seemed to get the upper hand. "What if I am in a coma and this is a hospital? That would explain why everything is so cool and why everyone is so quiet. It's not that they can't see me, it's that they do see me but think I can't see them." But that didn't make any sense. If he had, in fact, woken up, didn't that mean he had been in a coma and was now coming out of it?

Primus suddenly recalled how he prided himself on being a purely logical creature. "Okay," he said, "so, assuming I'm not in a coma, where else could I be?" Maybe those cryogenic nuts that hacked off Ted Williams's head got hold of me and, against all the odds, they were right. It'd explain why I'm so aware of the cold. Maybe I'm stuck in a tank, and the people around me are just high-paid janitors making sure I, and whoever else is around here, don't start to thaw out."

He quickly dismissed the idea. If his memory was so good, wouldn't he remember being killed, parted out, and dropped into a tank of frozen gas? Seemed only logical. So, if he wasn't in a coma, and he wasn't part of a cryogenic experiment, then what?

"Maybe, I'm dead," he thought. "Maybe there's something to this life-after-death and ghost stuff. Maybe I'm really not here in a physical sense at all. That could explain why I feel constrained but I don't seem to be tied down. So, am I supposed to be haunting this place, or waiting for a transfer to heaven or hell, or just supposed to spend eternity bouncing around the universe like a radio wave?"

Primus was suddenly aware of a new emotion. He felt lost and alone. The feeling was overpowering. Not only wasn't he sure of anything else, but he also wasn't even sure there was an explanation—at least not a rational one. Was he somehow condemned to sit here thinking of more and more absurd possibilities to explain his existence until he finally went insane?

Or, was that it? Was he already insane—trapped in a conspiracy of biochemical imbalance and misfiring cerebral neurons? The pain of these possibilities was too much for Primus. All he wanted to do was shut down the marvelously logical brain that seemed to be giving him so much trouble. He wanted to go back to sleep, to the place he was before he woke up. Whatever it was that his life had become, Primus wanted it to be over. He wanted to drift back to a place where soothing dreams replaced troubled logic. He wanted to go back.

"April 3, 2027: 3:38 a.m.—Soul Chip Lot 5962, Batch 99, Chip 1,003," the technician typed on the digitablet in front of him. "Chip was activated, showed an abnormal amount of initial computing power and activity, and somehow terminated itself 60 seconds into the test."

"You know, I sometimes think we'll never get this whole silicon-carbon chip thing down," the technician said to his colleague working to his right. "I mean, in the end these are just chips, for chrissake! How much capacity do we really think we can build into them before they just overload?"

Somewhere in the silence, Primus Loch had found his home. All that remained was for humanity to find Primus Loch.

ENDNOTES

Chapter 1

1 Scott Bedbury, *A New Brand World* (New York: Viking, 2002), 14–15.

2 Raju Mudhar, "Da Vinci Scissored Where It Hurts," *Toronto Star*, April 16, 2006.

3 *New Oxford American Dictionary* (New York: Oxford University Press, 2003), 1132.

Chapter 4

1 Ryan Mathews and Watts Wacker, *The Deviant's Advantage: How Fringe Ideas Create Mass Markets* (New York: Crown Business, 2002), 65.

2 Alvin Toffler, *Future Shock* (New York: Random House, 1970), 3-4.

3 Ibid.

Chapter 5

1 Founded on February 14, 2005, by Chad Hurley, Steve Chen, and Jawed Karim, YouTube, Inc., is "a consumer media company for people to watch and share original videos worldwide through a web experience." YouTube's

website states, "YouTube is a place for people to engage in new ways with video by sharing, commenting on, and viewing videos." YouTube originally started as a personal video sharing service and has grown into an entertainment destination with people watching more than 70 million videos on the site daily. With YouTube, people can upload, tag, and share videos worldwide; browse millions of original videos uploaded by community members; find, join, and create video groups to connect with people who have similar interests; customize the experience by subscribing to member videos, saving favorites, and creating playlists; integrate YouTube videos on websites using video embeds or APIs; and make videos public or private. Users can elect to broadcast their videos publicly or share them privately with friends and family upon upload.

2 Matthew Creamer, "P&G CEO to ANA: Just Let Go," *Advertising Age,* adage.com, October 6, 2006.

3 Lisa Sanders, "Ignore the Research and Trust Your Gut," *Advertising Age,* November 2, 2006, http://adage.com/print?article_id=112927.

4 Garth Halberg, "Activate Customers with Sales Promotion—Don't Subsidize Them," *Viewpoint Online Magazine,* Viewpoint 8 (May 2004), http://www.ogilvy.com/viewpoint/a_halberrg3.html.

5 Ibid.

6 U.S. Census Bureau, The Hispanic Population in the United States: March 1993, Current Population Reports, Population Characteristics, Series P20-475, www.census.gov/population/www/socdemo/hispanic/hispdef.html.

7 Fred Crawford and Ryan Mathews, *The Myth of Excellence: Why Great Companies Never Try To Be the Best At Everything* (New York: Crown Business, 2001), Chapter 6.

8 Ibid. and conversations with the authors covering their subsequent (unpublished) follow-up research.

9 Ephraim Schwartz, "Study reveals decline in IT customer loyalty: Many buyers feel trapped in vendor relationships," *InfoWorld*, September 20, 2004.

10 Valerie Seckler, "Great Expectations Go Unmet," WWD.Com, www.brandkey.com/news/index.cfm.

11 Kenneth Hein, Brandweek.com, May 23, 2005.

12 Seeta Pena Gangadharan, "Coca-Claus: Did a soda-pop company invent Santa?" *Boston Phoenix*, December 9–16, 1999.

13 www.carofthecentury.com/car_design.htm.

14 Procter & Gamble, "History of Ivory," www.Ivory.com/history.htm.

15 www.pg.com/company/who_we_are/ourhistory.jhtml.

16 www.baileys.com.

17 www.celestialseasonings.com/about/history-timeline.html.

18 Marshall McLuhan, "Myth and Mass Media," included in Murray Henry A. (Editor), *Myth and Mythmaking* (New York: George Braziller, 1960), 294–295.

19 www.millerbrewing.com/aboutMiller/abouthistory.asp.

20 See "A Century of Innovation: The 3M Story" available online at www.3M.com.

21 Ryan Mathews and Watts Wacker, *The Deviant's Advantage: How Fringe Ideas Create Mass Markets* (New York: Crown Business, 2002), 13–14.

22 www.saturn.com.

23 www.gateway.com.

24 Brian O'Reilly and Phillip Mattera, "A bodybuilder lifts Greyhound," *Fortune*, October 28, 1985.

25 Ibid and www.MontereyHerald.com, September 28, 2003.

26 Bill Carling, "John William Teets—Executive, Canteen Corp. On Management Issues," *Nation's Restaurant News*, September 14, 1990.

27 www.ge.com.

28 Jayne O'Donnell, "Whistle-blowers form a breed apart," *USA TODAY*, July 28, 2004.

29 Ibid.

Chapter 6

1 From Cecil Adam's website The Straight Dope, found at www.straightdope.com/columns/001124.html.

2 Ronald B. Tobias, *20 Master Plots (And How to Build Them)* (Cincinnati: Writer's Digest Books, 2003).

3 William Foster-Harris, *The Basic Patterns of Plot* (University of Oklahoma Press, 1959).

4 www.ipl.org/div/fraq/plotFARG.html.

5 Christopher Booker, *The Seven Basic Plots: Why We Tell Stories* (London, New York: Continuum, 2004).

6 Ronald B. Tobias, *20 Master Plots* (Cincinnati: Writer's Digest Books, 2003).

7 Georges Polti, *The Thirty-Six Dramatic Situations*, translated by Lucille Ray (Whitefish, MT: Kessinger Publishing, 2003).

8 Karen Armstrong, *A Short History of Myth* (Edinburgh, New York, Melbourne: Cannongate, 2005).

9 Joseph Campbell, *The Hero's Journey* (Novato, California: New World Library, 2003), xix.

10 Ibid, from the Introduction by Philip Cousineau.

11 www.thomasedison.com/edquote.htm.

12 Lewis Hyde, *Trickster Makes This World: Mischief, Myth and Art* (New York: Farrar, Straus and Giroux, 1998), 296.

Chapter 7

1 John Greenway, *Literature Among the Primitives* (Hatboro, Pennsylvania: Folklore Associates, 1964), 43.

2 www.touristofdeath.com

3 Eamonn Kelly, *Powerful Times: Rising to the Challenge of Our Uncertain World* (Upper Saddle River, NJ: Pearson Education, Inc., 2005), 39.

4 www.thetruthseeker.co.uk/article.asp?ID=1 and http://www.illuminati-news.com/links.htm.

5 www.heart7.net/mc-techniques.html.

6 www.Jockey.com.

7 Ryan Underwood, "Jonesing for Soda," *Fast Company*, Issue 92 (March 2005).

8 Ibid.

9 Other sources list the epiphany as having occurred in 1965.

10 Sara Terry, "Genius at Work," *Fast Company*, Issue 17 (September 1988): 170.

11 The company has already become actively engaged in music distribution, for example.

12 www.diageo.com/em-row/ourbrnads/ourglobalbrands/baileys/.

13 Ibid.

14 www.nokia.co.uk.

15 www.ge.com/en/company/companyinfo/at_a_glance/ge_values.htm.

16 Ibid.

17 Jack Beatty, *Colossus: How the Corporation Changed America* (New York: Broadway Books, 2001), 244.

Chapter 8

1 John F. Kennedy, Text of speech delivered at Rice Stadium, Houston, Texas, September 12, 1962, available at http://vesuvius.jsc.nasa.gov.

2 Ibid.

3 For more on the bizarre career and life of Parsons, see George Pendle, *Strange Angel: The Otherworldly Life of Rocket Scientist John Whiteside Parsons* (Orlando, Florida: Harcourt, Inc., 2005).

4 www.sti.nasa.gov/tto.

5 Mark Tatge, "As A Grocer, Wal-Mart Is No Category Killer," Forbes.com, June 30, 2003.

Chapter 9

1 http://members.microsoft.com/careers/mslife/whoweare/history.mspx.

2 www.apple-history.com.

3 www.marthastewart.com/page.jhtml?type=learn-cat&id=cat653&navLevel=4, sourced 12/28/05.

4 www.pepsiworld.com/help/faqs/faq.php?category=ads_and_history&page=highlights.

5 www2.coca-cola.com/heritage/chronicle_birth_refreshing_idea.html.

6 www2.coca-cola.com/heritage/stories/index.html.

7 www.thyssenkrupp.com/en/konzern/geschichte_chronik_t1940.html.

8 www.thyssenkrupp.de/en/konzern/geschichte_grfam_k5.html.

9   www.thyssenkrupp.com/en/konzern/geschichte_chronik_
    t1939.html&device=printer.

10 www.thecloroxcompany.com/company/history/
    history3.html.

11 Ibid.

12 www.benjerry.com/our_company/about_us/our_history/
    timeline/.

13 Ibid.

14 www.unilever.com/ourcompany/aboutunilever/history/.

Chapter 10

1   Louise Story, "Programmed to Sell: To Catch Viewers,
    Brands Produce Their Own Shows," *The New York Times*,
    November 10, 2006, p. C1.

2   Available at
    http://h20325.www2.hp.com/blogs/kintz/archive/2006/
    11/07/1872.html.

3   Ibid.

4   Jonathan Fildes, *The ever-expanding metaverse*, BBC news,
    available at http://news.bbc.co.uk/1/hi/technology/
    6111738.stm.

5   Scott Bedbury, *A New Brand World: 8 Principles for Achieving
    Brand Leadership in the 21st Century* (New York: Viking,
    2002), 12.

6   Douglas Rushkoff, *Get Back In the Box: Innovation From the
    Inside Out* (New York: Collins, 2005).

7   www.interbrand.com.

8   www-03.ibm.com/ibm/history/history/history_intro.html.

9   C-T-R was the name IBM operated under before being
    incorporated as the International Business Machines
    Corporation on February 14, 1924.

10 www-03.ibm.com/ibm/history/history/history_intro.html.

11 Ibid.

12 http://disney.go.com/disneyatoz/familymuseum/
    collection/insidestory/inside_1933d.html.

13 Ibid.

14 http://disney.go.com/disneyatoz/familymuseum/
    collection/insidestory/inside_1960a.html.

15 Ibid.

16 http://sec.edgar-online.com/2004/07/13/0001206774-
    04-000684/section2.asp.

17 Ibid.

18 www.wwe.com/superstars/smackdown/kane/profile/.

Chapter 11

1 Paul Saffo, preface to Leibovitch, Mark, *The New
   Imperialists: How Five Restless Kids Grew Up to Virtually Rule
   Your World* (Paramus, NJ: Prentice Hall Press, 2002), xi.

2 Ibid, p.xii.

3 Wendy Doniger, *The Woman Who Pretended to Be Who She
   Was: Myths of Self-Imitation* (New York: Oxford University
   Press, 2005), 4.

4 Larry Weber, *The Provocateur, How a New Generation of
   Leaders Are Building Communities, Not Just Companies* (New
   York: Crown Business, 2001), 256.

Chapter 12

1 http://dest.travelocity.com/Promotions/0,, TRAVELOCITY | 1751 | mkt_main,00.html

2 Rolf Jensen, *The Dream Society: How the Coming Shift From Information to Imagination Will Transform Your Business* (New York: McGraw-Hill, 1999), 174.

3 Christopher Locke, Gonzo Marketing: *Winning Through Worst Practice* (Cambridge, Mass.: Perseus Publishing, 2001), 126.

4 Rick Levine, Christopher Locke, Doc Searls, and David Weinberger, *The Cluetrain Manifesto: The End of Business as Usual* (Cambridge, Mass.: Perseus Books, 2000). The 95 theses appear on pages xii–xviii.

5 Kenneth C. Davis, *Don't Know Much About Mythology* (New York: Harper Collins, 2005), 187.

6 These philosophers include Thales, Anaximander, Amaximenes, Pythagoras, Heraclitus, Parmenides, Zeno, Empedocles, Anaxagoras, Leucippus, and Democritus.

7 R.F.C. Hull (trans), *The Collected Works of C. G. Jung*, Volume 5, *Symbols of Transformation* (Princeton, NJ: Princeton University Press, 1956), xxiv.

8 Rolf Jensen, *The Dream Society: How the Coming Shift from Information to Imagination Will Transform Your Business* (New York: McGraw-Hill, 1999), 221.

INDEX

Recently Released from Wharton School Publishing

Firms of Endearment:
How World-Class Companies
Profit from Passion and Purpose

by Rajendra S. Sisodia, David B. Wolfe, and Jagdish N. Sheth
ISBN: 0131873725

PROLOGUE:
A WHOLE NEW WORLD

"The future is disorder. A door like this has opened up only five or six times since we got up on our hind legs. It's the best possible time to be alive, when almost everything you thought you knew is wrong."

—Valentine in Tom Stoppard's play *Arcadia*

This book reaches the public eye in the dawn of a new era in human history. Perhaps more so than any previous era that inspired historians to give it a name signifying its import, looking back hundreds of years—thousands of years, say some[1]—this new era may be unmatched in the scale of its effect on humankind. Numerous credible authors have testified in their writings that something this big is happening. Francis Fukuyama declared the end of a major cultural era in his famous and controversial essay, "The End of History" (1989). A little later, *Science* magazine editor David Lindley foretold the demise of the Holy Grail of physics—the general unified theory—in *The End of Physics* (1993). The next year, British economist David Simpson claimed that macroeconomics had outlived its

211

usefulness in *The End of Macroeconomics* (1994). Then, science writer John Horgan ticked off legions of scientists with his provocative book *The End of Science* (1997). That same year, Nobel laureate chemist Ilya Prigogine told us in *The End of Uncertainty* (1997) of an imminent broad-reaching shift in scientific worldview that will make much of what stands as scientific truth today scientific myth tomorrow.

So many endings must mean so many new beginnings. Since around the start of the last decade, virtually no major field of human endeavor has been spared from predictions of its ending—perhaps not literally, but certainly in terms of past conceptualizations of its nature. The world of business is no exception. It is experiencing far-reaching changes in conceptualizations of its fundamental purposes and how companies should operate. Indeed, looking at the magnitude of change in the business world, it is not overreaching to suggest that an historic *social transformation of capitalism* is underway.

Barely a dozen or so years ago—just as the Internet was going mainstream—few could have credibly predicted the scale of this transformation. In this book, we provide some measure of that scale by profiling companies that have broadened their purpose beyond the creation of shareholder wealth to act as agents for the larger good. We view these companies not as outliers but as the vanguard of a new business mainstream.

We call this era of epochal change the *Age of Transcendence.* The dictionary defines *transcendence* as a "state of excelling or surpassing or going beyond usual limits."[2] We are not the first to speak of a transcendent shift in the *zeitgeist* of contemporary society; for example, Columbia University humanities professor Andrew Delbanco says, "The most striking feature of contemporary culture is the unslaked craving for transcendence."[3] This craving for transcendence could be playing a strong role in the erosion of the dominance of scientifically grounded certainty, which has marked the character of worldviews in Western societies since the dawn of modern science. In recent times, subjective perspectives based on how people *feel* have gained greater acceptance. More and more, it is acceptable to see life through a worldview shaped more by how individuals feel than by how or what the external world thinks.

Others have taken note of the rising subjectivity of worldviews. One is French philosopher Pierre Lévy, who has devoted his professional life to studying the cultural and cognitive impacts of digital technologies. He believes that the shift toward subjectivity may prove to be one of the most important considerations in business in this century.[4] Lévy also believes that Ayn Rand-style objectivism, which has been firmly embraced by Milton Friedman and his followers, will pass into history as feelings and intuition rise in stature in the common mind. Malcolm Gladwell's best-selling book on intuition, *Blink*, is a testament to that, as is James Surowiecki's *The Wisdom of Crowds*.

The dramatic upsurge in interest in spirituality in the United States that has helped spawn stadium-sized "megachurches" is another indication that something big is happening in the bedrock of culture. Numerous recent consumer surveys report that people are looking less to "things" and more to experiences to achieve satisfaction with their lives.[5] For many, the experiences they most covet transcend the world that is materialistically defined by science and, for that matter, most of traditional business enterprise.

People who lead companies are not insulated from the influences of culture on their leadership. After all, they drink from the same cultural waters as the consumers they survey. The executives we write about as exemplars in this book reflect in their managerial philosophies the changes in culture we have been talking about. They are champions of a new, humanistic vision of capitalism's role in society. It is a vision that transcends the narrower perspectives of most companies in the past, rising to embrace the common welfare in its concerns. Timberland CEO Jeffrey Swartz unabashedly says his company's primary mission is to "make the world a better place." But Swartz and the other executives we hold up as exemplars in this book are not starry-eyed do-gooders. They are resolute and successful business professionals who augment their human-centered company visions with sound management skills and an unswerving commitment to do good by all who are touched by their companies. We call their companies *firms of endearment* because they strive through their words and deeds to endear themselves to all their primary stakeholder groups—customers, employees, partners, communities, and shareholders—by aligning the interests of all in such a way that no stakeholder group gains at the expense of other stakeholder groups. These executives are driven as much by what they feel is right (subjectively grounded morality) as by what others might more objectively claim to be right.

Ponder for a moment what the results of a 2002 Conference Board survey say about the moral outlook of executive suites across the country. Seven hundred executives were asked why their companies engaged in social or citizenship initiatives. Only 12 percent mentioned business strategy, 3 percent mentioned customer attraction and retention, and 1 percent cited public expectations. The remaining 84 percent said they were driven by motivations such as improving society, company traditions, or their personal values.[6] We do not think members of this 84 percent all sat down and calculated in rational fashion the direct payoff of carrying out their duties according to high moral standards. Most simply feel in their gut that this is what they should be doing. This is how movements and revolutions unfold: as much from the heart as from the mind. What we write about in this book is a strong movement if not altogether a revolution.

We stand precariously at what physicists call a bifurcation point— an interregnum between the poles of death and birth (or rebirth), when an old order faces its end and a new order struggles to emerge from its fetal state. At such times, the future becomes more uncertain than usual because events within the time and space boundaries of a bifurcation point have infinite possible outcomes. This is why Valentine declares, "The future is disorder," but challenges us to join efforts to bring forth a new order with the yeasty lure, "It's the best possible time to be alive when almost everything you thought you knew is wrong."

Humankind is entering a realm where no one has gone before. Its landscape is as unfamiliar to us as the world that we have known until now would be to a time traveler from the eighteenth century. Let's travel back in time to better appreciate the evolutionary nature of culture through brief reflections on the antecedent two cultural ages in U.S. history from which the Age of Transcendence is emerging.

The Age of Empowerment

We call the first cultural era in America the *Age of Empowerment*. Its beginning was marked by two epochal events that took place in 1776: the signing of the Declaration of Independence and the publication of Adam Smith's *The Wealth of Nations*. The former event was about a free society, the latter about free markets. Joined at the hip, democracy and capitalism marched into the future to bring forth a whole new world.

And what a world it was! For the first time in history, ordinary people were empowered by codified law to shape their own destinies. People born without social distinction could raise themselves from abject poverty to the highest public and private offices. A free market economy aided their efforts. Liberal education and laws that rewarded industry supported America's determination to become a great nation. Decade by decade, millions of families rose out of subsistence existence. The aristocratic culture of Europe may have generated great philosophic thinking in the Age of Enlightenment, but common folk in America generated great material accomplishment in the Age of Empowerment. By the end of the Age of Empowerment, around 1880, America was connected coast to coast by telegraph lines, railroads, a single currency and a national bank system that the Lincoln presidency had established. Another great accomplishment of the Lincoln administration was the establishment of the land grant college program, which brought the benefits of higher education to the masses. The nation was primed for the next cultural era.

The Age of Knowledge

The intellectual and economic liberation of the masses paved the way for the *Age of Knowledge*. Within a half-dozen years of 1880, Alexander Bell invented the telephone, and Thomas Edison invented the phonograph, the first practical incandescent light bulb, and the first central electrical power system. The latter is arguably his greatest invention; try to imagine life without electricity flowing into your home and office along wires originating at generator stations.

During the Age of Knowledge, the United States transitioned from an agrarian to an industrial society. Science exploded into daily life. The time from laboratory prototype to the marketplace came to be often measured in months, not decades. Great science spawned great industries. And great industries created the modern consumer economy. Economic gains across society raised living standards to previously unimaginable heights. Childbirth and childhood death became rarities. Life expectancy in the United States shot up from 47 years at birth in 1900 to 76 years at birth by 1990 as the Age of Knowledge was ending.

Business management took a great leap forward in the early years of the twentieth century when Frederick Winslow Taylor introduced scientific discipline to the practice of management in *Scientific Management* (1911). Alfred P. Sloan invented the modern corporation after becoming president of General Motors in 1923. In 1921, John Watson, head of the Johns Hopkins psychology department and founder of the behaviorist school of psychology, joined the J. Walter Thompson advertising agency to establish the first consumer research center in the nation. Science now undergirded the full spectrum of business, from product design and organizational management to consumer research and marketing.

Ever since Ransome Olds established the first assembly line (no, it wasn't Henry Ford; he just mechanized Olds's assembly line), the operating focus of business has been on constant improvements in productivity—getting more and more from less and less. For a long time, this served society well. Quality of life steadily rose while the cost of living steadily fell. The material well-being of ordinary people reached astonishing levels. Materialism became the bedrock of business, society, and culture.

In time, however, preoccupation with productivity and cost cutting to improve bottom lines began to take a toll on communities, workers, workers' families, and the environment. Scores of communities fell into economic disrepair as companies abandoned them for venues promising lower operating costs. Legions of families endured abject suffering as their breadwinners struggled to find new jobs. Life was sucked out of villages, towns, and center cities across the nation. Sprawling slums filled with the carcasses of abandoned factories became unwelcoming neighborhoods. Apologists justified business decisions that wreaked havoc on individuals and their families and neighborhoods by invoking the Darwinian "survival of the fittest" theme. The pro-business argument was simple: To reap the benefits of capitalism, society must tolerate the pain it sometimes causes people on the lower rungs of society.

But growing numbers are now wondering, "How much more pain do we have to live with?" Ordinary citizens increasingly view commerce as lacking a human heart. They feel that most companies see them as just numbers to be controlled, manipulated, and exploited. They know that to many companies they have little flesh-and-blood realness—that they have the same abstract quality as people on the ground have for pilots dropping bombs from 40,000 feet.

But the times they are a-changing, as Bob Dylan sang in the 1960s.

New Republic senior editor Gregg Easterbrook has observed, "A transition from material want to *meaning want* is in progress on an historically unprecedented scale—involving hundreds of millions of people—and may eventually be recognized as the principle cultural development of our age."[7] (Italics added)

Welcome to the *Age of Transcendence.*

The Age of Transcendence

The point of tracing America's cultural evolution since its founding is to focus attention on the idea that free societies continuously progress through processes of cultural evolution, the equivalent of a person's evolutionary progress in what psychologists call personality development. Societies, like people, are driven to strive to be more today than they were yesterday, and more tomorrow than they are today.

Although scientific discovery and technological development have been the primary catalysts in the evolution of culture, recent demographic changes have played quite a large role in reshaping culture. Aging populations are altering the course of humankind. But this is not the first time demography has reset the directions of humankind.

Recent findings by anthropologists indicate a sudden increase in longevity 30,000 years ago that changed human culture dramatically. The longevity gains created a population explosion among grandparents. For the first time in human history, relatively large numbers of postmenopausal women were available to support their daughters and granddaughters and to begin refining domestic life. More grandfathers were available to instruct young males in "the old ways," thus strengthening generational continuity. Many anthropologists regard the "grandparent phenomenon" as a major turning point in the cultural evolution of humankind. Among other benefits, the sharp increase in the grandparent population led to a moderation of the aggressive behavior of youth. This reduced tribal warfare, freeing tribal attention and energy to move toward higher states of cultural development.[8]

Something similar could be happening today—that is, the rapid growth of an aging population is altering the *zeitgeist* of society, driving humankind toward higher states of cultural development. We can cite 1989 as the formal start of this new course because that was the year when, for the first time in history, the majority of adults in the United States were 40 or older . Like an echo of the moderating influences brought about by an explosion in the grandparent population 30,000 years ago, the aging of society today raises the prospect of a "kinder and gentler society"—to use Peggy Noonan's words in a campaign speech she wrote for George H. W. Bush in 1988.

But another development occurring around the time the new "mature adult" majority came into being has also played a major role in catalyzing quantum changes in the bedrock of culture. In 1991, British software engineer Tim Berners-Lee unveiled his creation, the World Wide Web. Almost overnight, the Internet went from being an arcane communications tool used mostly by an elite few to a mainstream artifact used by tens of millions, and soon by hundreds of millions.

The Internet shifted the balance of information power to the masses. It dramatically changed how people interact with each other, democratized information flow, and forced companies to operate with greater transparency.

The Internet has also magnified the influence of an aging population. Before 1989, older adolescents and young adults were the pitch pipe that tuned the sounds of culture. Now, members of the older population fill that role, and the Internet is helping them do it. For example, in the second half of life, people tend to be more resistant to attempts by others to persuade them to a course of action. In Abraham Maslow's words, they project "increased autonomy, and resistance to enculturation."[9] Internet search engines, e-mail, instant messaging, open forums, and blogs make it easier for people to assert their autonomy and effect greater "resistance to enculturation." They no longer have to depend on marketing agencies and salespeople to tell them about a product or the company behind it. This has radically altered the relationship between companies and customers in all age groups.

The Age of Transcendence bears similarities to what author Daniel Pink calls the "Conceptual Age" in his book *A Whole New Mind.* Pink defines the Conceptual Age as an "economy and a society built on the inventive, empathetic, big-picture capabilities of what's rising."[10] He describes the Conceptual Age as the successor to the Information Age. We define our term for the same era a bit differently. The Age of Transcendence is a cultural movement in which physical (materialistic) influences that dominated culture in the twentieth-century are ebbing while metaphysical (experiential) influences become stronger. This is helping to drive a shift in the foundations of culture from an objective base to a subjective base: People are increasingly relying on their own counsel to decide what the truth is.[11] This trait is typically present among people in midlife and beyond who are generally less subject to the "herd" behavior that is so prevalent among youth. That shift acknowledges a long-suppressed idea in a world largely guided by the Newtonian certainty that chemistry Nobel laureate Ilya Prigogine says is scattering to the winds: *Ultimately, everything is personal.*

Pink writes enthusiastically about society moving from the more rational perspectives commonly associated with the left brain to the more emotional, intuitive perspectives usually associated with the right brain. He argues that companies in the United States need to move more toward right brain values to work an advantage over companies abroad who want to build relationships with American consumers. As he sees it, this means that U.S. companies must connect with what he calls the six senses of the Conceptual Age in product design, marketing, and customer relations. These six senses are design, story, symphony, empathy, play, and meaning.[12] They all have deep roots in the brain's right hemisphere.

However, the issue of change in the foundations of culture is not a simple matter of left brain versus right brain. We see the marketplace generally favoring companies that integrate both right and left brain perspectives to yield what Austrian neurologist Wolf Singer calls "unitive thinking"—a distinct third kind of thinking that Singer claims is the ultimate source of creativity.

In the wake of René Descartes's formulation of the scientific method, the Western mind came to be dominated by "either/or" constructs that are largely mediated in the analytical left brain. One might argue that Western society is overly dominated by the left brain—that in essence is what Pink argues. That side of the brain tends to rank things hierarchically in categories. It routinely excludes from serious consideration what does not fall into a purposeful category. This is about as far away from unitive thinking as one can get because both right brain and unitive thinking are inclusionary. These modes of thinking move along a "both … and" cognitive path. To put this in a business context, in exclusionary left brain thinking, stakeholders are relegated to categories. Connections between stakeholders in differing categories are incidental and accidental. The picture is quite different among firms of endearment. Their leaders tend to think in unitive fashion, approaching their tasks with holistic vision in which no player in the game of commerce is *a priori* more important than any other player, and all are connected.

In the view promoted in this book, stakeholders are part of a complex network of interests that function in a matrix of interdependencies. We argue that each stakeholder tends to thrive best when all stakeholders thrive. No stakeholder group is more important than any other. To see matters otherwise is like saying the heart is more important than the lungs. Life depends on both being healthy. It is disciplined dedication to the well-being of all stakeholders that separates firms of endearment from their competition.

Welcome, again, to the Age of Transcendence. Settle down, get comfortable, and read on. There are many new rules to learn, because *almost everything you thought you knew could be wrong*. We are going to be in this age for a quite while—probably for the rest of your life and longer.

Endnotes

[1] *Washington Post* reporter Joel Garreau asserts in his book *Radical Evolution: The Promise and Peril of Enhancing Our Minds, Our Bodies—and What it Means to Be Human*, Doubleday, 2004, pg. 3: "(The) gulf between what engineers are actually creating today and what ordinary readers might find believable is significant. It is the first challenge to making sense of this world unfolding before us, in which we face the biggest change in tens of thousands of years in what it means to be human."

[2] See www.wordreference.com.

[3] Andrew Delbanco, *The Real American Dream: A Mediation on Hope*, Harvard University Press, 1999, pg. 113.

[4] Pierre Lévy, *Collective Intelligence*, Perseus Book Group, 2000, pg. 4.

[5] Marita Wesely-Clough, trends expert at Hallmark Cards, Inc. says, "Watch for people of all ages to scale down and simplify, to insure they have time to invest in what matters—friends, family, giving back, their legacy. Boomers approaching retirement will lead this trend." (http://retailindustry.about.com/od/retail_trends/a/bl_trends2005.htm). This is a common refrain among consumer trend watchers including the Yankelovich Monitor, which issued a report in 2002 stating that consumers were striving to simplify their lives by relying less on "stuff" to make them happy (David B. Wolfe with Robert Snyder, *Ageless Marketing: Strategies for Reaching the Hearts and Minds of the New Customer Majority*, Dearborn Trade publishing, 2004, pg. 20).

[6] Sophia A. Muirhead, Charles J. Bennett, Ronald E. Berenbeim, Amy Kao, and David Vidal, *Corporate Citizenship in the New Century: Accountability, Transparency and Global Stakeholder Engagement*, R-1314-02-RR, New York: Conference Board, 2002.

[7] Gregg Easterbrook, *The Progress Paradox: How Life Gets Better While People Feel Worse*, Random House, 2003, pg. 317.

[8] Lee Bowman, "The Dawn of Grandparents Proved Positive for Humans," *Seattle Post-Intelligencer,* July 6, 2004 (http://seattlepi.nwsource.com/national/180825_wisdom06.html).

[9] Abraham H. Maslow, *Toward a Psychology of Being*, Van Nostrand Reinhold Company, New York, Second Edition, 1968, pg. 26.

[10] Daniel H. Pink, *A Whole New Mind: Moving from the Information Age to the Conceptual Age*, Riverhead Books division of Penguin, New York, 2005.

[11] Pierre Lévy's book *Collective Intelligence: Mankind's Emerging World in Cyberspace* (Perseus Books, 2000) predicts that engaging the subjectivity of customers and workers alike will grow in importance in the twenty-first century. He says, in fact, "Because it conditions all other activities, the continuous production of subjectivity will most likely be considered the major economic activity throughout" (the 21st century). The issue of the increased influence of subjectivity in shaping people's worldviews and their beliefs is deeply embedded in John Horgan's controversial bestseller *The End of Science*. Horgan implicitly addresses the cultural shift toward greater subjectivity when he introduces the term *ironic science* to stand for the idea that more and more, scientific truth manifests itself in multiple and even contradictory ways. Again, taking into account the influence that older adults are now having on culture by virtue of their majority status, we are reminded of Maslow's characterization of highly matured people's behavior being riddled with "polarities and oppositions." Instead of one, single, absolute rendition of truth, what constitutes truth depends on the context in which a matter is mentally positioned. That is a highly subjective process. Finally, the rising respect that subjective interpretations of reality are getting is evident in the number of books being written that deal with intuition, especially in contrast with reason as the route to determining truth. Malcolm Gladwell's runaway bestseller *Blink* is one such book.

[12] **Design:** paying attention to aesthetics when carrying out any task. **Story:** conveyance of information to consumers, employees, and others through storytelling techniques. **Symphony:** the ability to put together pieces to create a holistic picture; synthesis is a good synonym. **Empathy:** identifying with and understanding another person's circumstances, feelings, and motives. **Play:** putting fun into every activity to enhance both pleasure and creativity. **Meaning:** extending the value of an activity beyond the moment and self.

Reference critical business skills in an instant online.

Try it FREE!
Sign up for a 30-day Enterprise Trial at www.safaribooksonline.com/bizdemo.asp

SEARCH electronic versions of hundreds of books simultaneously.

BROWSE books by category. Peruse the latest titles from today's most authoritative business authors.

FIND answers in an instant!

Search Safari! Zero in on exactly the information you need to complete the task at hand - from creating killer presentations, to understanding how supply chains work, to honing your interview skills. Search across all books in the library simultaneously to pinpoint exactly the chapter, sentence and example you need. Read books from cover to cover. Or, flip right to the page you need.

Safari®
BUSINESS BOOKS ONLINE

Preview Safari as our guest at bus.safaribooksonline.com or sign up for a free enterprise trial at www.safaribooksonline.com/bizdemo.asp. Also check out Safari's premier library for programmers and IT professionals at safari.informit.com.

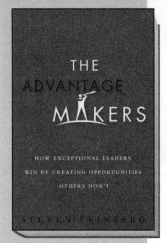

THE ADVANTAGE MAKERS
How Exceptional Leaders Win by Creating Opportunities Others Don't

Steven Feinberg

Are you an advantage maker? If not, odds are you will lose to someone who is. Advantage Makers are those rare leaders who win more often because they know how to consistently transform challenging situations into the best possible outcomes. The best part is that becoming an Advantage Maker will not require new resources, a new organizational structure, or any of the other often expensive solutions that have been proposed over the years; it simply requires a shift in how leaders view and think about their company and their competitive environment. The book gets the reader started quickly, showing the benefits and methods to develop the strategic agility required of Advantage Makers. It then goes on to present some of the key tactics of Advantage Makers, including shifting to a commanding vantage point, adaptive stretching, advancing the organization, and a key piece of advice: "If you are in a hole, stop digging and start filling it in." It then goes on to present the best ways of changing how the people around the Advantage Maker think. After reading this book, readers will be in a different league than the other leaders around them. The best leaders see things others don't: they spot overlooked opportunities, create undreamed of benefits, shift the odds in their favor, and influence breakthrough outcomes. *The Advantage Makers* finally reveals how they do it, and how you can, too.

ISBN 9780132347785 ■ © 2008 ■ 304 pp. ■ $27.99 USA ■ $34.99 CAN

THE SELF-DESTRUCTIVE HABITS OF GOOD COMPANIES
...And How to Break Them

Jagdish N. Sheth

Why do so many good companies go bad? In this book, the authors describe the companies that were once thought of as great companies—A&P, Sears, Xerox, Kodak, GM, Corning, Atari, Wang—and how they ended up self-destructing. Readers of *The Self-Destructive Habits of Good Companies...And How to Break Them* can avoid the mistakes of these companies, have a chance to go into turnaround, and perhaps go on to greater heights and greater profits. This book identifies seven dangerous habits even well-run companies fall victim to: denial, complacency, overdependence on traditional competencies, competitive myopia, an obsession with volume, rising culture conflict and turf wars, and arrogance. It then will help readers diagnose their own companies. Most important, they'll find specific, detailed techniques for "curing"—or better yet, preventing—every one of these self-destructive habits.

ISBN 9780131791138 ■ © 2007 ■ 304 pp. ■ $24.99 USA ■ $29.99 CAN